9780486232003
AF573928

TWENTY-TWO *Authentic Banquets* FROM INDIA

COMPILED BY

ROBERT H. CHRISTIE

DOVER PUBLICATIONS, INC.

New York

Contents

Copyright © 1975 by Dover Publications, Inc.
All rights reserved under Pan American and International Copyright Conventions.

Published in Canada by General Publishing Company, Ltd., 30 Lesmill Road, Don Mills, Toronto, Ontario.
Published in the United Kingdom by Constable and Company, Ltd., 10 Orange Street, London WC2H 7EG.

This Dover edition, first published in 1975, is an unabridged and unaltered republication of the Indian and Afghanistani sections of *Banquets of the Nations,* published by J. & J. Gray and Co., St. James Press, in 1911. A new Publisher's Note has been written specially for the present edition.

International Standard Book Number: 0-486-23200-X
Library of Congress Catalog Card Number: 75-9173

Manufactured in the United States of America
Dover Publications, Inc.
180 Varick Street
New York, N.Y. 10014

Publisher's Note

The measures in this book are British. Dry measures and measures of weight correspond fairly closely to American, but liquid measure is based on the Imperial standard, which is about 20% larger than the American. (An Imperial gallon is thus roughly equivalent to 5 American quarts.) In small quantities this difference is not significant; a little less liquid than the recipe calls for will usually be satisfactory. In cases where large quantities of liquid are used, however, this 6/5 ration must be borne in mind.

Preserves should be prepared following traditional American methods.

The following ingredients may be unfamiliar or unobtainable.

Asafoetida. Very strong; sample before using.

Bombay duck. Small dried fish used as a condiment or seasoning. No real equivalent.

Cardamoms. The distinction between black and white cardamoms need not be observed.

Castor sugar. Granulated sugar.

Chilli. For red chillis use crushed red peppers (Capsicum); for green chilli Italian peperoncini may be used. ½ teaspoon equals about 1 chilli.

Cochineal. Substitute red food coloring.

Cocoanut milk. If bottled cocoanut milk is not available, follow the recipe on page 60, substituting dried cocoanut; figure about 1 cup of dried cocoanut per cocoanut.

Coriander leaves. Obtainable in Chinese grocery stores; Italian parsley may be substituted.

Curd. For most recipes cottage cheese can be used, although yoghurt can be used in recipes that call for acid-soured milk. For boiled-down sweet milk, condensed milk may be substituted.

Dal. Lentils, particularly peeled, halved seeds. Commercial brown lentils are acceptable.

Garam masalla. A mixture of spices, recipe on page 118.

Ghee. Generally speaking, ghee (or ghi) is butter with the casein removed so that the butter does not scorch in cooking. To make ghee, place the butter in a pan of water and let the water come to a boil for a few minutes. Remove from the fire and let it cool. When the butter hardens, remove it from the water; the casein will be suspended in the water. The cook, however, can always substitute butter for ghee. Specialty shops which carry Indian food supplies often sell bottled ghee.

Ginger. By green and white ginger the author means fresh ginger root, which is peeled, then grated, sliced, or pounded. Obtainable in Chinese grocery stores; otherwise substitute half the quantity of powdered ginger, though this is not so good. Lump ginger is whole dried ginger.

Goat meat, kid. Substitute lamb.

Gram, gram flour. The Indians have a much richer variety of dried beans than we do, gram being a generic term for a legume. Any form of bean flour may be used; try health food shops. If you have a flour mill or an electric grinder, it may be used. Bengal gram is chick peas.

Horseradish tree fruit. No equivalent. Try zucchini.

Lady fingers. Okra.

Lemon grass. Obtainable in Chinese, Indonesian supply houses; you can substitute basil.

Lemon leaves. Substitute a twist of lemon peel.

Lentil flour. Try health food stores or substitute soy or other bean flours, although they will not be as good.

Linseed oil. Do not use commercial linseed oil, which contains unwholesome or poisonous additives. Substitute sesame oil, from health food stores.

Musk. Possibly obtainable from an old-fashioned druggist, but best omitted.

Mustard oil. Probably unobtainable. Substitute peanut oil; a teaspoon of mustard seed may be cooked in a cup of peanut oil to simulate the flavor.

Nasturtium leaves. From your flower garden, or substitute a few pickled capers.

Prawns. Shrimp.

Rawa. Substitute fine bulghur from health food or Near Eastern stores.

Silver leaves. Best omitted.

Tamarinds. Tamarind juice and tamarind jelly are usually obtainable in Chinese or Near Eastern food stores. In cooking a lesser quantity of guava jelly may be substituted; for chutneys, fresh peaches are a good substitute.

Wheat, coarse ground. Bulghur of various grades from health food or Near Eastern stores.

Yeast. Follow the proportions by weight indicated on dried yeast package; the yeast recipe on page 151 is unreliable.

I

BENGAL (Hindu)

Menu

Ghee
(Clarified Butter)

Mussoor Dāl
(Lentils)

Gheevhāt
(Spiced Rice)

Kātol
(Curried Turbot)

Rohit
(Fried Salmon)

Bende Kāvi Sāru
(Curried Lady's Fingers)

Jhāl Chāi
(French Beans)

Begoon Bhāhjā
(Fried Egg Plant)

Dāl Pithas
(Lentil Croquettes)

Khimān
(Minced Meats)

Kabutār Doopiajas
(Stewed Pheasants)

Shandēsh
(Milk Balls)

Cajure
(Sweet Wheaten Cakes)

Hālwa Sond
(Milk Pudding)

MUSSOOR DAL. (Fried Red Lentils.)

Wash and pick half a pound of red lentils; when thoroughly dry, roast the same as you would coffee beans. Now put into a pan one ounce of tamarinds, three teaspoonfuls of ground onions, one teaspoonful of ground large red chillies, half a teaspoonful of turmeric, half a teaspoonful of ground green ginger, a quarter teaspoonful of ground garlic, and a half teaspoonful of salt, the roasted lentils, and sufficient water to stand two inches above the mixture. Give it a good stir, then place it on the fire till the lentils are all dissolved, being careful not to disturb the contents till they are cooked into a soft mass. Now take and whip the mass with a wire whisker (in lieu of a churn) till quite light, removing the tamarind seeds during the process. Cut a pound of onions in slices, not too thin, and fry till a reddish brown in two ounces of boiling ghee. Heat six ounces of ghee in a pan; chop up the onions, which, along with the lentils, put into the ghee. Place the pan on the fire and stir well, and simmer at the side of the fire for twenty minutes. Eat with vegetables. fish, and meats.

GHEEVHAT. (Spiced Rice).

Slice two onions very fine and fry in four ounces of ghee till dark brown, but not charred, then put in four cloves, six cardamoms, a teaspoonful of coriander, half a teaspoonful of caraway, and a pounded red chilli, and fry for two or three minutes. Put this into a pan with a pound of well-washed rice and thirty ounces of water and three teaspoonfuls of salt. Boil till all the moisture has evaporated, and place at the side of the fire to dry. Eat with fish, vegetables, and meats.

KATOL. (Curried Turbot.)

Cut two pounds of turbot into two-inch squares, free of skin and bones. Mix a teaspoonful each of ground turmeric, coriander, and cumin, and brown in boiling ghee. Pour in one teacupful of boiling water and half a teaspoonful of salt, and boil for five minutes ; add a stick of cinnamon, and one point of garlic, and boil for other two minutes. Eat with plain boiled or spiced rice, lentils, and chutnies.

ROHIT (Fried Salmon.)

Cut two pounds of salmon into two-inch squares, free of skin and bones. Smear the pieces with a mixture composed of a teaspoonful each of ground coriander and ground onions, half a teaspoonful red chillies, and one and a half teaspoonfuls of salt. Let stand for an hour. Cut three large onions into very fine slices, and fry a rich brown in six ounces of boiling ghee ; place them to the one side and fry the pieces of salmon ; just before finishing add the fried onions. Eat with bread, rice, and fish chutnies.

Bende Kavi Saru. (Curried Lady's Fingers.)

Wash twenty-four lady's fingers, rub the skin with a rough cloth to remove all bristles, cut in inch lengths, wash a second time in water, and dry them.

In a pan fry four or five large sliced green chillies and one red chilli in boiling ghee, a few sliced onions, one point of crushed garlic, a pinch of mustard seeds, and a pinch of caraway seeds. Drain and fry your pieces of lady's fingers in the above, and add a cup of cocoanut milk and two of curds; cover very carefully, and allow to simmer till the vegetables are soft and tender. Add salt to taste just before dishing. Eat with lentils, rice, ghee, and pickled cucumbers.

Jhal Chai. (French Beans.)

Fry a couple of sliced onions in two ounces of mustard oil till a nice brown, and remove to the one side, then fry one teaspoonful of red ground chillies, a teaspoonful of coriander, the same quantities of ground turmeric and ground onions. Now put in a pound of French beans broken in two and the strings carefully removed, also a teaspoonful of salt, three ounces ghee, and a cupful of water. Simmer very gently till the beans are cooked. Eat with dal pittas, ghee, lentils, rice, and other vegetables.

Goli (Cauliflower.)

Is cooked the same way, only breaking the flower into small branches.

Begoon Bhahja. (Egg Plant.)

Wash and slice two pounds of the plant into pieces rather less than a quarter of an inch thick. Wipe them with a dry cloth and fry in two ounces of boiling mustard oil, first having steeped them for an hour in a teaspoonful each of ground cinnamon, ground coriander, red chillies, a pinch of saffron, and salt to taste. Eat with dal, rice, and chutnies.

Dal Pithas. (Lentil Croquettes.)

Fry six sliced onions in boiling mustard oil, lay on the one side, and fry two teaspoonfuls of ground onions, half a teaspoonful ground red chillies, half a teaspoonful of ground ginger, half that quantity of ground garlic, a teaspoonful of coriander seeds, a quarter of a teaspoonful of aniseed. Put to the one side the fried condiments, &c. Having washed a quarter-pound of lentils, steep them for four hours, dry them thoroughly, and fry in the mustard oil, and put in a pot with the fried condiments, with just sufficient water to cover the ingredients, adding a very small teaspoonful of salt. Simmer very slowly for about half-an-hour, or until a soft mass.

(If to be eaten with another dish the sliced fried onions should be strewn over the top.)

Roll out rather thinly a piece of dough much the same as puff paste, and cut out rounds with a cutter about five inches in diameter. Place a spoonful of the above mixture when cold in the centre of each round, wet the edges, fold over, and fry in boiling mustard oil or ghee. They are shaped like a half-moon. Eat with rice, chutnies, and other vegetables.

KHIMAN. (Minced Meat.)

Bring to the boil two ounces of ghee, in which fry a large onion finely minced; now put in two pounds of kid which has been passed through a fine mincer, and fry till well browned, stirring all the time; then add four green chillies and an inch of green ginger, both thinly sliced a ground red chilli, half a teaspoonful of salt, and a large cupful of water. Stew very gently for an hour, then mix a teaspoonful of flour with a little water, and stir it into the mince along with a large tablespoonful of tamarind juice.

For the British table, beef, mutton, lamb, or veal may be cooked the same way, the only seasonings, however, being salt, pepper, and onion. In Scotland this dish is known as "minced collops."

KABUTAR DOOPIAJAS. (Stewed Pheasants.)

Cut a plump young pheasant into eight pieces. Fry in three ounces of boiling mustard oil four large onions sliced very thin, and when of a reddish yellow place to one side. Then fry in the same oil four teaspoonfuls of ground onions, one teaspoonful of turmeric, and one teaspoonful of red chillies. When browned, fry the pieces of pheasants, and pour in two tablespoonfuls of water, the fried onions and condiments, and one teaspoonful of salt. Eat with bread, or rice and chutnies.

SHANDESH. (Milk Balls.)

Bring to blood heat three pints of milk, put in a tablespoonful of whey or a tablespoonful of essence of rennet, and stand till all the milk has solidified. Now place in a towel and hang up till nothing but the dry curd is left. Mix this with a little rice flour, and make into round balls about the size of a tennis ball. Boil sugar and water till nearly candy high, *i.e.*, till it is quite sticky, remove from the fire, and when lukewarm put in the curd balls, and stand for a day. Strain, dish, and eat with cream (milk reduced to quarter its weight by boiling).

CAJURE. (Sweet Wheaten Cakes.)

Mix well one and three-quarter ounces of well-washed roughly-ground wheat, two tablespoonfuls of melted butter, a pound of sugar, and a pound and three-quarters of milk. Now add sufficient flour to make a good dough· Knead well and lay to the one side for four hours, after which take pieces and make into small cakes about the size of a five shilling piece, and fry in boiling ghee.

HALWA SOND. (Milk Pudding).

Put a quarter-pound each of brown sugar, butter, and milk in a pot, and mix well together, and place on the fire till bubbles come out, then put it on a dish, pour a little ghee or butter over, and sprinkle sliced almonds on top. It should be a soft semi-solid mass.

Green Mango Chutney.

Peel a couple of large green mangoes, stone and cut in pieces, and steep in cold water for an hour. Pound the flesh to a smooth pulp, and mix in two tablespoonfuls of sugar, then add a quarter teaspoonful of ground red chillies, half a teaspoonful of ground mint, and the same quantity each of ground green ginger and salt. Mix thoroughly.

Potato Chutney.

Slice a large onion very finely, also two green chillies. Mix with the juice of a fresh lime a tablespoonful of milk curd, a ground red chilli, and salt to taste. Meanwhile boil eight potatoes, previously cleaned and skinned, mince them rather finely, and mix in the onions, chillies, and lime juice.

Fish Chutney.

Mix onions, chillies, and lime juice as in potato chutney. Roast a quarter-of-a-pound of the small dried fish known as " Bombay ducks," then roughly pound; stir in half a dessert-spoonful of mustard oil, and add the onions, chillies, and lime juice, and just a suspicion of garlic in place of the milk curd.

Egg Plant Chutney.

Roast a couple of good large egg plants, remove the seeds, and pound the flesh to a smooth paste with a teaspoonful each of mustard oil and salt, and then mix with onions, red chillies, curd, and lime juice, as given in potato chutney, only using two limes instead of one.

Tamarind Chutney.*

Stone two pounds of ripe tamarinds and put in a glazed pot with two ounces each of ground red chillies, garlic, and green ginger, one ounce of ground cinnamon, four ounces of cleaned currants, four ounces of sultana raisins, two ounces salt, one pound of soft sugar, and one pint of vinegar. If not enough of the latter to cover all the ingredients, add more. Put on a good fire to stew fairly quick. Care must be taken to stir continuously the contents of the pan till the mixture is thick. Remove from the fire, and when cold it can be bottled for future use.

*This chutney is very hot; much less chilli could be used.

II

BENGAL (Mussulman)

Menu

Hilsa Coftā
(Curried Herring Balls)

Chingri Doopiajas
(Prawn Curry)

Murgi Pulau
(Pillau of Chicken)

Bharā Hussānee
(Grilled Fillets of Lamb)

Kabutār Doopiajas
(Stewed Pheasant)

Gora Quormā
(Curried Beef)

Puras no Mālāhi
(Cream Croquettes)

Zurdā
(Egg Sweet)

Sheer Mhāll
(Honey Cake)

Dhāi
(Milk Curd)

Hulluah
(Wheat Milk Tablet)

HILSA COFTA. (Curried Herring Balls.)

Pound the flesh of one pound of herrings to a pulp, mix with it half a teaspoonful of salt, white pepper and ground coriander, a pinch of cloves, a teaspoonful of ground onions, and a tablespoonful of tamarind juice. Mix well and make up into balls rather larger than a walnut.

Bring to the boil four ounces of mustard oil, and fry the following for three minutes :—Half an ounce of ground onions, a tablespoonful of ground green chillies, quarter teaspoonful of pepper, half that quantity of garlic, half a dessert-spoonful of fine herbs, and when browned put in the balls and fry them on all sides. Add a little salt and a small cupful of water, and simmer slowly till cooked. Eat with fish chutney and rice.

Herrings pickled in tamarind juice is very similar to hilsa.

CHINGRI DOOPIAJAS. (Prawn Curry.)

Wash a dozen large prawns, parboil, remove from the shell, and lay to the one side. Then fry in ghee four teaspoonfuls of ground onions, one teaspoonful of ground turmeric, and one teaspoonful of ground large red chillies. When brown, put in the prawns and brown. Now add a cupful of water and the fried onions roughly chopped, and one teaspoonful of salt. Close the pot and stew till the prawns are cooked. Eat with rice or bread and fish chutney.

MURGI PULAU. (Pillau of Chicken.)

Clean a good fat chicken. Put it in a pot with two large cupfuls of water, a large onion cut in four, a small piece of ginger, and salt to taste. Boil till tender, but not too soft. Fry in four ounces of ghee twelve onions finely sliced till they are a nice brown, taking care not to char. Remove the onions and fry in three ounces of butter half a pound of well-washed rice. When the rice has taken up all the butter, add four cloves, four cardamoms, four sticks of cinnamon, two coriander leaves, two blades of mace, and three teaspoonfuls of salt. Give it all a good stir, and pour over the stock the fowl was boiled in, along with a cupful of milk which has been boiled to half its bulk; add one red and three green chillies sliced, and a handful of sultana raisins. Cover the pot carefully, and stew very slowly on a gentle fire (which ought to be allowed to go down) till all the moisture is nearly absorbed, being careful to give the mixture a stir now and again to keep it from charring. Cut the chicken into eight pieces and fry in oil till a nice brown, place on a dish and cover with rice, first removing the coriander leaves, the mace, and as much of the cinnamon as possible; heat the fried onions and strew on the top. Garnish with hard-boiled eggs cut in quarters.

BHARA HUSSANEE. (Grilled Pickled Lamb.)

Take two pounds of lamb and cut into fillets about an inch square. Thread six of these alternatively with a slice of green ginger and onions on thin pieces of bamboo or ordinary skewers. Prepare the rest of the meat the same way till all is used.

Boil six ounces of ghee, and brown in this one teaspoonful of turmeric, half a teaspoonful of green ginger, half a teaspoonful of caraway, four teaspoonfuls of ground onions, and half a teaspoonful of ground red chillies. Then brown the fillets and pour in half a cupful of curd, the same quantity of water, and one ounce of salt. Bring to the boil, and simmer gently at side of fire till meat is tender. Eat with rice and chutnies and luchi bhaja.

LUCHI BHAJA. (Wheaten Flour Cakes.)

Make a dough of flour, water and ghee; knead well. Form into small balls, flatten out with the hands, and fry in ghee. Eat when cold with meats.

GORA QUORMA. (Curried Beef.)

Fry in two ounces of mustard oil four onions finely sliced. When brown lay to the one side, and fry for two minutes in the oil a teaspoonful each of ground turmeric, coriander, and cumin, half a teaspoonful each of cinnamon, caraway, and cloves, a ground red chillie, a teaspoonful of salt, a point of garlic; and then fry two pounds of beef cut into inch squares and about half-an-inch thick. Put all the above in a pot with a large cup of sweet milk curd, the same of water, two bay leaves, two lemon grass leaves, three sliced green chillies, the juice of a lemon, and, if need be, a little more salt. Stir all the ingredients and cover the pan very closely and stew very gently on a slow fire for about an hour, or till the meat is tender, then stir in two tablespoonfuls of ghee. Remove the bay and lemon leaves, and eat with rice, luchi bhaja, and all kinds of chutnies.

KABUTAR DOOPIAJAS. (Curried Pheasants.)

Proceed exactly in the same way as in Hindu recipe.

PURAS NO MALAHI. (Cream Croquettes.)

Take two pounds six ounces of good milk, and reduce to half its bulk by boiling ; set to the one side to get cold. Mix with the yolks of four eggs 7 dwt. 12 grains of ground small cardamom and four ounces of sugar, and beat till pretty stiff, then beat in the cold milk and make into small round cakes, and fry in plenty of boiling ghee.

ZURDA. (Egg Sweet.)

Take of well-switched eggs half a dozen, of sugar quarter of a pound, ghee half a pound, blanched and split almonds two ounces, cinnamon in small pieces one and a half grains, suffron one grain, and rose-water one and a half ounces.

Fry the cinnamon and almonds in the ghee. Boil the sugar to a very strong syrup. Now add the ghee, almonds, and cinnamon, and bring to the boil. Remove the pot from the fire, stir in the saffron and well-beaten eggs, whipping all the time. When practically cold stir in the rose-water.

SHEER MHALL. (Honey and Almond Cake.)

Mix one pound of flour with one pound of soojee (the thick liquid of rough-ground wheat soaked in water for several hours squeezed through muslin) and two pounds of milk; knead well into a good dough. Melt down ¾ of an ounce of yeast in a little milk saved from the two pounds. Mix this with the dough along with one ounce of ghee and a little salt. Put it in a warm place to rise for two hours. Form the dough into shapes, place on a baking iron, and set to rise for another two hours, then smear on the top some good honey, sprinkle with roughly chopped cleaned almonds, and bake in a good oven.

DHAI. (Milk Curd.)

Put four pounds of good milk on to boil till it is reduced to one pound. When nearly cold beat it together so that the cream and milk are well mixed.

HULLUAH. (Wheat Milk Sweet).

Wash one and a half pounds of roughly ground wheat, and steep in three pounds of water for twelve hours. When quite soft strain through fine muslin, pressing all the good out. In the liquid stir in one and a half pounds of sugar; stir till it thickens with the boiling. Now put in six cardamom, six sticks of cinnamon, and a good pinch of saffron into eight ounces of boiling ghee and fry for three minutes, and stir it into the thickened sugar along with some pistachio nuts and sultana raisins. Place on the fire, and keep stirring till it again thickens. Pour into an oiled deep dish, and cut into strips about an inch broad.

III

BOMBAY (Brahmin)

Menu

Chutnies
(Bean, Cocoanut, Onion, Pomegranate, Raddish)

Kadhi
(Bean and Buttermilk Soup)

Dal
(Lentil Soup)

Ghee
(Clarified Butter)

Bātātāchi Bhāji
(Curried Potatoes)

Gujarāchi Bhāji
(Curried Carrots)

Āmbat Chorka
(Curried Sorrel)

Bhhajiyā
(Curried Cakes)

Bhāt
(Rice)

Dāl
(Lentils)

Shrikhand
(Milk Curd and Fruit)

Bāsūudi
(Spiced Milk)

Jalebi
(Sweet Macaroni)

Keshri Bhāt
(Sweet Rice)

Bhāt ne Dāhi
(Rice and Curd)

Bean Chutney.

Soak four ounces white beans overnight, drain and pound to a paste. Bring two ounces oil to the boil and fry a quarter teaspoonful of mustard seeds ; when these are crackling, remove from the fire at once ; put them in the bean flour along with a teacupful of curds, a tablespoonful tamarind juice, one red and three green chillies finely sliced, one ounce of pistachio nuts, a teaspoonful of brown sugar, and half a teaspoonful of salt. Cook for three or four minutes, and serve when cold.

Onion Chutney.

Roughly grate a pound of onions, and add to them two cups of milk curds, the juice of a lemon, half a teaspoonful of pounded mustard seeds, a teaspoonful of brown sugar, and half a teaspoonful of salt ; mix well. It should be a moist, soft mass.

Radish Chutney.

Clean and finely shred a pound of white radish roots, in which mix a cupful of milk curds, a half teaspoonful each of ground mustard seeds, cumin seeds, coriander seeds, brown sugar, and salt. It should be soft and moist.

Cocoanut Chutney.

Grate half a cocoanut roughly, and mix with it a teaspoonful of sugar and sufficient curds to make all into a soft mass.

POMEGRANATE CHUTNEY.

Remove the seeds to weigh about a pound, and mix them with four ounces of milk curds, one teaspoonful brown sugar, and a good pinch of white pepper.

KADHI. (Bean and Buttermilk Soup).

Take one pound of gram flour (bean or white pea flour will do), which put in a pot with two pounds of good buttermilk, a teaspoonful of turmeric, and same quantity of salt. Boil till the whole is of the consistency of very thin porridge.

DAL. (Lentil Soup).

Wash two pounds of lentils and put in a pot with same weight of water; add a tablespoonful of curry powder, and a large teaspoonful of salt. Cook till the whole mass is like very thin porridge.

CURRY POWDER.

One ounce turmeric, one ounce coriander seeds, one ounce cumin seeds, half ounce yellow mustard seeds, quarter ounce each of poppy seeds and aniseed, two ounces of cardamom, half ounce of garlic, one ounce of green ginger, one ounce of large green chillies, and half an ounce of large red chillies. Put the pot in a cool oven till all the ingredients are dry, then pound till all will go through a fine sieve.

BATATACHI BHAJI. (Curried Potatoes.)

Peel two pounds of potatoes and cut them into half-inch pieces, boil in water in which you have put a teaspoonful of mustard seed, a shred red chilli, and a large teaspoonful of salt. When the potatoes are soft, drain, and pass through a sieve. Put in a tablespoonful of white pease flour, and a little of the water in which the potatoes were boiled. Bring all to the boil, stirring all the time so that the potatoes and flour amalgamate.

Now boil two ounces of oil, in which fry quarter teaspoonful of mustard seeds, and when they are crackling and dancing, be sure that you remove the pan from the fire at once. Pour this into the potato mixture, and stir well over the fire so that it is hot. The whole should be the consistency of soft porridge.

GUJARACHI BHAJI. (Carrots.)

Take two pounds of carrots and treat them the same way as the potatoes, with the addition of half a teaspoonful each of pounded coriander and cumin seeds.

AMBAT CHORKA. (Curried Sorrel.)

Wash and shake slightly a pound of sorrel leaves. Put them in a pot with little or no water, a sliced red chilli, two sliced green ones, half a teaspoonful each of ground coriander, cumin, and turmeric, and a teaspoonful of salt; and when the leaves are tender, drain and put through a sieve, then add the mustard seeds cooked as in potato curry.

BHHAJIYA. (Curried Cakes of Gram Flour.)

Make a thickish liquid paste of quarter pound gram flour with milk, then add two ounces ghee, one-eighth ounce each of assafœtida, coriander, cardamom, cumin seed, ground pepper, and chillies, and a quarter-ounce of salt. After mixing them well and making a thick liquid paste, with a spoon drop small quantities into plenty of boiling ghee, and when well browned lift out with an open skimmer. They should be in lumps about the size of walnuts.

DAL. (Lentils.)

Wash and clean two pounds of lentils; put in pot with water, with a teaspoonful of turmeric, and same quantity of salt, or more if required. Cook until the whole is in a semi-solid state.

BHAT. (Rice.)

Clean one pound rice in two waters. Put it in a pot with furiously boiling water—the water to be standing two inches over top of rice. Remove to the side of fire to boil slowly till all water evaporated and rice dry.

SHRIKHAND. (Milk Curd and Fruit.)

Put three pounds of sweet milk curd in a muslin bag and hang up to drain overnight, then mix in three pounds of sugar, and pass all through a very fine sieve. Take twenty grains pounded saffron, mix well with four ounces milk, which add to the curds and sugar along with a tablespoonful each of raisins, peeled almonds and pistachios, and make all into one mass. It should be a semi-solid mass, and is eaten with bread as a separate dish.

BASUNDI. (Spiced Milk.)

Put three pounds of milk and three pounds of sugar in a pan, and reduce to nearly half its volume. When cold, stir in twenty grains powdered saffron and a small pinch of nutmeg, which have been well mixed in four ounces of good milk. This is served in small bowls as a drink, or eaten with soft bread dipped into it.

JALEBI. (Sweet Macaroni.)

First of all prepare rawa as follows:—Wheat is washed and laid on a cloth for four or five hours to dry. Then it is ground. Then the coarse flour produced is rubbed over a cloth, through which the finer material passes. The residue is shaken on a basket. The husks and colouring matter separate, and the granules which remain are known as rawa.

One pound rawa, two ounces ghee, one and three-quarter ounces of rice powder, and one and a quarter ounce of lentil powder, are mixed with water and milk so as to form a thin liquid, and the juice of one or two lemons (according to size) added. The whole is mixed in the evening and allowed to stand overnight.

In the morning two pounds of sugar with enough water to form a sticky liquid is boiled. This solution is called pak.

The preparation which has stood overnight is then rubbed in a pot until it forms a paste so adhesive that the pot may be lifted by taking hold of the contents. It has now become too thick to pour, so milk must be added and whipped till it froths.

Then a kettle containing one pound of ghee is put on a slow fire ; when this boils, the paste is poured into it from a cocoanut shell with a hole as large as a big pea in it, or is squeezed through an ice piping cloth. In pouring the paste the hand is carried round and round in such a way that the paste forms circular masses of coils, which at once solidify in the boiling ghee. These masses are then placed in the hot pak, and after a little time removed on to a sieve or strips of wood and allowed to drip.

Green Mango Jelly.

Made the same as guava jelly, only the mangoes have to be steeped for thirty-six hours, and no lime juice is added to the jelly. Eat with parentha.

Mango Cheese.

Made the same as guava jelly, omitting the lime juice.

Apricot Marmalade.

Stone and skin the fruit. Scald it in an earthenware jar, then pound to a paste. Take equal weight of pulp and soft sugar, and boil for fifteen minutes, stirring all the time and being careful to remove all scum. Put into pots whilst hot, and tie down when cold.

Plum Marmalade.

All kinds of plums may be preserved as above.

Bhat ne Dahi (Rice and Curd).

Proceed as in "Bhat": mix half a teaspoonful of ground saffron in two cups of curds, and stir into the rice.

IV

BOMBAY (Mussulman)

MENU

Rāhu Mooloo
(Stewed Carp)

Bunihui Māchli
(Steamed Salmon)

Boi Cutlse
(Shrimp Croquettes)

Chow Chow Pullao
(Chicken Pillau)

Seik Kāwāb
(Grilled Pickled Lamb)

Kichri
(Curried Mutton)

Bāsundi ne Puri
(Cream and Pancakes)

Solā
(Vermicelli Pudding)

Bundee
(Sweet Balls)

Mo-Rubbā
(Guava Preserve)

Huluā
(Spiced Wheaten Sweet)

Phul
(Fresh Fruits)

RAHU MOOLOO. (Stewed Carp.)

Cut two pounds of carp free of skin and bones into two-inch pieces; rub them very thoroughly with a mixture of salt, green ginger, and red chillies (of each a spoonful), and put to the one side for an hour; then dry them and fry in boiling ghee till cooked, and put to the one side till cold. Fry in four ounces of boiling ghee three finely sliced onions to a light brown colour; place to the one side and fry in the same ghee a chopped green chilli, a teaspoonful of coriander, turmeric, and aniseed (of each a teaspoonful), a little white pepper, and a teaspoonful of diluted cocoanut milk. Stir over the fire till dry; then add the fried onions, a cupful of good cocoanut milk, the juice of a lemon, and more salt if necessary. Pour the hot sauce over the cold fish, and serve with puri, chapatee, chutnies, etc.

BUNIHUI MACHLI. (Steamed Salmon.)

Rub two pounds fillet of salmon with a teaspoonful each of ground salt, coriander, and chillies. Fry in six ounces of ghee six onions sliced very thin (they must be of a light brown). Then put in the fish. Close very tight so that no air can get in. Put the pan in a pot of water (bain marie) which comes half way up the pan, and boil gently for half an hour. The water should boil very slowly. Eat with chapatee (new bread) and chutnies.

This is the nearest approach to the native fish rowe or roa.

CHAPATEE. (Pulled Bread.)

Make a good dough of flour and water, knead it well, after which take it in the hands and pull it for a considerable time; then take a piece rather less than a tennis ball, and with the hands clap it till it is about an eighth of an inch thick, and bake on an iron plate, turning when one side is done.

BOI CUTLSE. (Shrimp Croquettes.)

Take one pound of shrimps, wash thoroughly, and boil with salt, a sliced red chilli, a piece of green ginger, half ounce coriander seeds, and a point of garlic. When cooked remove the shells, etc., and roughly chop the meat.

Fry in three ounces ghee two finely sliced onions till browned, but not charred; put to the one side; and fry one teaspoonful of ground coriander, half a teaspoonful of ground aniseed, and half a teaspoonful of ground cumin seeds; now put in the chopped shrimps, with rather less than half a teaspoonful of salt, and fry lightly; mix onions (chopped very fine), condiments, and shrimps, and put on a dish till cold.

Prepare a good puff paste, roll out thin, and cut into rounds about the size of a small saucer. Take as much of the shrimp mixture as would make a walnut, and place in the middle of one of the rounds of pastry; wet the edges and put another on the top, and press closely. Fry in boiling ghee, and eat with pulled bread.

Or the round of paste may be cut larger and the

mixture placed in the centre. After wetting the edges, fold over, press the edges closely, and fry.

Chow Chow Pullao. (Chicken Pillau.)

Cut a chicken into eight pieces, and fry in a pan in which you have first browned, in boiling ghee, a large onion cut in dice. Put it in a pot along with a cupful of curds, a cupful of water, a teaspoonful each of ground coriander and cardamoms and half that quantity of cloves and caraway, a saltspoonful of white pepper, and a teaspoonful of salt.

Boil three quarters of a pound of rice and a quarter of a pound of yellow peas till half cooked ; strain, and stir this into half a pound of boiling ghee and some more seasonings. Cook for a minute or two ; then put it in the pot with the chicken, along with four ounces of cleaned and split almonds, four ounces of dry white grapes, and a teaspoonful of saffron. Stir all together, and close the pot very closely, and cook till meat, etc., are tender. There should be very little moisture, but add more water if necessary, as great care must be taken that no charring takes place.

Eat with bread, and any of the vegetables as cooked in Brahmin recipes.

Seik Kawab. (Grilled Pickled Lamb.)

Put in an earthenware dish four teaspoonfuls of ground onions, one teaspoonful of ground large red chillies, half teaspoonful of ground green ginger, half teaspoonful of poppy seeds, one teaspoonful of ground coriander seeds, a pinch of saffron, a good pinch of ground cloves, one and a half teaspoonfuls of salt, four ounces of milk curd, juice of a lemon, two tablespoonfuls of mustard oil, and a little melted butter (ghee). Give all a good stir so that they may be thoroughly mixed.

Cut two pounds of lamb into neat squares of about two inches, score them deeply on both sides (do this in opposite directions so as to avoid cutting right through the pieces), and pickle in the above mixture for two hours, turning repeatedly so that all the meat will absorb the mixture. Dry and thread these squares on to a sufficient number (six on each) of thin pieces of bamboo or ordinary skewers, and grill, basting as often as possible with ghee mixed with a little of the liquid in which they were pickled. Before serving take them off the skewers, and eat with bread, such as chapatee, phulka, etc., and chutnies.

KICHRI. (Curried Mutton.)

Cut two pounds of mutton into quarter-inch squares. Fry in four ounces ghee (melted butter) two large onions cut in thin slices ; when light brown, place to the one side, and fry for two minutes in the same ghee a teaspoonful each of turmeric, coriander, aniseed, and cardamoms, half that quantity of garlic, cinnamon, cloves, and green ginger, a red chilli, and some salt. Add more ghee, and fry a large cupful of washed rice, and the same quantity of lentils. Fry the pieces of mutton lightly on both sides. Put meat, onions, condiments, rice and dal all together in a pan; pour in two cupfuls of water and half a cupful of ghee. Mix all together, and bring to the boil; then place the pan at the side of the fire to cook slowly till the meat is tender. Add more water if the mixture is too dry.

May be eaten with bread and any of the vegetables and chutnies given in the Brahmin dinner.

BASUNDI NE PURI. (Cream and Pancakes.)

BASUNDI.

Reduce four pints of milk to a quarter its bulk by boiling, and add to it one pound castor sugar. After it gets a bit cool, add three ounces of almonds thinly sliced, a quarter ounce of cardamoms, and two ounces of "chironzia sapida" seeds (roughly chopped almonds will do equally well). It is served cold in the form of a thick liquid paste, and eaten with puri.

PURI.

Knead well half a pound of wheat flour with water, butter, and two ounces castor sugar. Roll out the paste and make about a dozen pancakes of it, and fry them on both sides in butter till they get brown in colour.

SOLA. (Vermicelli Pudding.)

Steep some vermicelli till soft, then fry in plenty of ghee; when it is cooked, stir in sufficient sugar syrup to make very sweet. Stir on the fire till it is all a soft firm mass; then colour with saffron; add some pieces of pineapple cut small, and pour into a dish. Eat when cool.

BUNDEE. (Sweet Balls.)

Take half a pound of rough wheat flour, and cook in sufficient ghee (melted butter) until it forms into small pellets by continuous moving with a spoon. Boil four ounces of sugar with the same quantity of ghee which you put into the flour, till it is a liquid. Then add the pellets and boil till it takes a solid form, and let it cool. When cold enough roll into balls (with the hands) about the size of tennis balls, and eat when cold.

MO-RUBBA. (Guava Preserve.)

Peel and quarter some ripe guavas. Steep in water for an hour. Put them in a preserving pan and just cover with water ; boil for an hour, or till in a soft mass. Strain through a jelly bag overnight. Now put the juice in the pan again and boil for fifteen minutes ; then add enough sugar to sweeten, but not to deaden altogether the tartness of the fruit. Skim carefully, add the juice of five limes to every fifty guavas, and boil for half an hour, or till clear of scum. Pour into jars whilst hot, and cover closely when cold.

GUAVA CHEESE.

Pass the pulp of the guavas, from which you have made the jelly, through a sieve, and add the juice of a lime to every three quarters of a pound weight of pulp. Boil slowly till quite thick, colour with cochineal, then pour into buttered pots and dry in a cool oven.

Hulua. (Spiced Wheaten Sweet.)

Make a syrup of half a pound of sugar. Brown half a pound of well-washed roughly ground wheat. Bring half a pound of ghee to the boil, and fry the wheat along with half a dozen cardamoms and three or four sticks of cinnamon. Keep the ingredients moving all the time. When lightly browned, stir in the syrup, and keep stirring till all becomes a thick mass. Pour on to a dish, and cut into neat pieces.

V

BURMAH

Menu

Ameh-tha-Nat
(Stewed Beef)

Gnāh-Jaw
(Roast Fish)

Cha-Zan-hin-jaw
(Pork and Macaroni)

Hmō Jaw
(Roasted Mushrooms)

Chet-tha-hin
(Stewed Chicken)

Woon-beh-oo-jaw
(Ducks' Eggs Roasted)

Gnāh-Pee-goung
(Minced Fish, Chillies, etc.)

Woon-beh-jaw
(Stewed Duck)

Pa-Zoon-hin
(Roast Prawns)

Tha-yet-thee-chin
(Pickled Fruit)

Tho-tha-jaw
(Fried Mutton)

Thayet thee
(Stewed Mangoes)

Zithei
(Stewed Plums)

AMEH-THA-NAT. (Stewed Beef.)

Wash twice two pounds of beef, and cut it into little pieces. Have half-a-teaspoonful of chillies, one teaspoonful onions, quarter teaspoonful saffron, and half a teaspoonful salt, ground and fried in five ounces lard. Put in the meat and fry it. Then pour in some water, and when it is dried up add some curds and a little water, and when reduced to nearly four ounces dish and serve with boiled rice and pickled fruits.

RICE.

A thick cut of bamboo about three inches in diameter and eighteen inches long is half filled with rice, and water poured in till it stands three inches over the rice. The bamboo is then slung at an angle of 45 degrees on a tripod over a fire till all the water is evaporated, when the rice should be ready.

GNAH JAW. (Roast Fish.)

Steep two pounds of strongly cured dried fish, skin uppermost, in some milk for four hours. Take the skin off and free from bones, and mince it finely. Take half a teaspoonful of ground mild chillies, half a teaspoonful of cumin, quarter teaspoonful of nutmeg, one teaspoonful of ground onions, a pinch of pepper, and the pulp of two tomatoes reduced by boiling in oil. Make the whole, when mixed, into cakes the size of a five shilling piece. Roast in the oven, and when finished put a few drops of unsweetened lime juice on each cake. Serve with rice and sliced raw cucumber.

CHA-ZAN-HIN-JAW. (Pork and Macaroni.)

Take two pounds of good fresh pork, cut it into inch squares, and fry in lard. Parboil and drain some broad macaroni cut into one-inch lengths. Put the meat and macaroni in a pan, and add four ounces dried mushrooms, a handful of nasturtium leaves, a tablespoonful of olive oil, and some softened split yellow peas, pepper and salt, a dust of flour, a teaspoonful each of turmeric, cumin, and coriander, and two pints of water. Cook very slowly for an hour and a half. The moisture must be very little, and the meat tender and succulent. Eaten with rice and pickles.

HMO JAW. (Roasted Mushrooms.)

Clean well and skin some medium-sized mushrooms. Make a mixture of pounded onions, salt, pepper, and olive oil. Smear the underside of the mushrooms with this, and cook in oven till tender.

CHET-THA-HIN. (Stewed Chicken.)

Clean a plump chicken and truss as for boiling. Rub it over with a mixture of pepper, salt, saffron, pounded chillies, pounded onions, sesamum oil, cardamoms, and cinnamon, and let stand for two hours. Place a sliced carrot and a slice of fried pork in the bottom of a pot. Put in chicken, add half a pint of water and half a pint of stock, and stew slowly till tender. Reduce the stock to a semi-glaze, and pour over. Add more salt if necessary, and serve with rice.

Woon-beh-oo-Jaw. (Duck's Eggs Roasted.)

Heat some oil in a pan; add a quarter teaspoonful salt, one teaspoonful of pounded onions, half a teaspoonful of pounded chillies, and one teaspoonful of pounded cardamoms. Fry for a couple of minutes, then drop the eggs in one by one. Dish when cooked. Eat with pickles.

Gnah-Pee-goung. (Minced Fish, Chillies, &c.)

Clean some strongly cured fish from all skin and bones, and mince finely. Pound some large chillies and onions, and put in a dish with a plentiful supply of oil and roast. Serve with rice and picked vegetables dried and dressed with sesame oil and a little soy. The higher the fish the better the dish (*sic!*).

Woon-beh-jaw. (Stewed Duck.)

Bone a good fat duck without breaking the skin; pour into it a mixture made of a teaspoonful each of mustard, sesame oil, and soy. Make a gravy of the bones and giblets, seasoning it with pepper, salt, soup-herbs, and a few bay leaves. Mince together with the liver of the duck two pounds and a half of good beef, half a pound of beef suet, a dessertspoonful of chopped garden herbs, a teaspoonful of grated bread-crumbs, a teaspoonful of curry powder, a sliced apple, and a teaspoonful each of black pepper, salt, and sugar. Mix these well together, and stuff the duck. Put three ounces of good oil in a pot, and when hot, put in the duck along with a quarter of a pound of curdled milk, four steeped and stoned green mangoes, and six potatoes cleaned and quartered; pour over the giblet gravy, and allow it to cook until tender. Eat with rice, pickles, and chutney.

PA-ZOON-HIN. (Roast Prawns.)

Shell one dozen large prawns, after parboiling them. Put two ounces of oil into a frying-pan till hot, then put in two teaspoonfuls of ground onions, half teaspoonful each of ground chillies and turmeric, and a pinch of ground garlic. When brown add the prawns and three quarters of a teaspoonful of salt, and fry them brown. Eaten with plain boiled rice and mixed pickles dressed in oil.

THA-YET-THEE-CHIN. (Pickled Fruit.)

Wipe dry some different kinds of plums, cherries, grapes, and any other small fruits which are not quite ripe. Boil sufficient very good vinegar to cover, adding a teaspoonful of turmeric, same of coriander and cumin seeds, half teaspoonful of cinnamon and half that quantity of caraway, and half a salt-spoonful of cayenne pepper, to every quart of vinegar. When boiled up, pour over the fruits, which you had placed in jars, and when cold cork very tightly, and cover the latter in a couple of days with wax or bladder.

THO-THA-JAW. (Fried Mutton.)

Two pounds of mutton, two tablespoonfuls of lard, two teaspoonfuls of coriander seed, one and a half teaspoonfuls of salt, half tablespoonful curry powder, pinch of cayenne pepper, the same of white pepper, one small onion, one sour salted lime, six sour and salted plums, and three teacupfuls of water.

Pound the coriander, salt, curry powder, cayenne, and onion, into a semi-solid paste, which fry in melted lard in a hot stew-pan for a minute, but do not let it char. Then put the meat (already washed in cold water and cut in small pieces) in the lard, stirring till it is thoroughly browned. Put in the water and the sour lime and sour plums, which have been pounded into a smooth mass, close the lid on the pot, and stew on a slow fire for one and a half hours, or till tender. The gravy left at the end of the cooking should be reduced to one cupful. Serve with boiled rice.

If any vegetable is to be added to the meat, then it should be fried with the meat and undergo the same process as the meat. Skinned potatoes cut in quarters are the best.

THAYET THEE. (Stewed Mangoes.)

Steep a dozen green mangoes in water for thirty-six hours. Drain thoroughly, and put them in a pan with strong sugar syrup, and stew till tender.

Zithei. (Stewed Plums.)

Wash and dry thoroughly and stew in the oven or at the side of the fire in a strong sugar syrup till tender but not pulped.

Mixed Pickles.

To every two quarts of the very best vinegar put one and a half ounces of white ginger, scraped and sliced, the same of long pepper, two ounces of peeled shallots, one ounce peeled garlic, one and a half ounces salt, one ounce turmeric, one ounce coriander, half ounce mace, pinch of cayenne, and one ounce mustard seeds. Boil for a few minutes. Have ready a shred white cabbage and a cauliflower broken into small branches, some small white radishes, young French beans (stringed), small gherkins, and small silver onions. Pour boiling brine over them, and let steep for three days. Drain and dry in a cloth, and then thoroughly dry on a sieve in front of the fire. Place this in bottles with the vinegar. Keep uncorked for two days, and put more vinegar in when required, as the vegetables must be completely covered. Cork and seal with wax to exclude all air.

VI

CENTRAL PROVINCES (Brahmin)

MENU

Bhāt
(Rice)

Dāhl
(Lentils)

Ghee
(Clarified Butter)

Aloobhāt
(Curried Rice and Potatoes)

Sém
(Broad Beans)

Bādre
(Curried Tomatoes)

Wilpussān Chāhkee
(Curried Turnips)

Mutter Chāhkee
(Green Peas)

Dāhl Falooree
(Spiced Lentil Crusts)

Kārānji
(Cocoanut Croquettes)

Sa-oo Bhāhjees
(Baked Apples)

Shrikhānd
(Sugared Cream)

Hulluāh
(Cinnamon Sweet)

Bhat. (Rice.)

Wash the rice thoroughly, and, having put it in a pot, add water until it reaches a level about three inches higher than the rice. Boil until rice is soft, then cover the pot and leave it on the hot embers until the fire dies out. No water is poured off, and nothing else is added.

Dahl. (Lentils.)

First boil the water, and when fully boiling put in some split lentils and allow them to become soft. After putting in the lentils, and when boiling point is again reached, add a little turmeric powder. Allow the contents to simmer half an hour, stir well, add hot water, and some salt.

Aloobhat. (Curried Rice and Potatoes.)

Half pound of rice, one pound potatoes. Wash rice well, and cut potatoes into thin slices. Put rice in four ounces boiling ghee, stir a little, and then take out. Put a thin layer of this rice in a pot, and place upon it a thin layer of raw potato. Again rice and again potato, and so on until material is used up. Put the pot upon a slow fire. Another pot full of water is placed upon the first, so that the vapour from the first may condense and fall back into the lower pot. Finally salt, chillies, cloves, and cinnamon are added on removing from fire.

SEM. (Curried Beans.)

Wash and steep in clean water two pounds of red or white beans (haricot) for twelve hours ; strain and fry lightly in four ounces of boiling linseed oil in which you have first fried a teaspoonful of mustard seeds ; add one teaspoonful each of cumin, coriander, and turmeric, a very little green ginger, one sliced green chilli, one ground red chilli, a large cupful of water, and a teaspoonful of salt, and stew till the beans are quite tender. Use the water that the beans were steeped in for the stewing. Eat with rice, bread, ghee, chutney, etc.

SULTANA CHUTNEY.

Soak one pound of sultana raisins in thirty ounces of good vinegar till quite soft. Take them out and pound to a soft mass. Now put the vinegar back, along with twelve ounces of sugar, three ounces each of ground green ginger, garlic, and salt, three quarters of an ounce of ground red chillies, and twenty-four almonds blanched and split. Mix all well together, and bottle.

BADRE. (Curried Tomatoes).

Plump two pounds of tomatoes in boiling water for a minute, then remove the skins and cut in quarters. Bring to the boil two ounces of refined linseed oil, in which fry a teaspoonful of mustard seeds till they are dancing ; then put in the tomatoes, two ounces of melted ghee, a teaspoonful each of salt, turmeric, coriander, and red chillies, a squeeze of lemon, and a pinch of sugar. Stew till the moisture is nearly reduced to nil. Eat with ghee, chapatee, rice, lentils, and chutnies.

MANGO PICKLE.

Peel and half split fifty unripe mangoes. Remove the stones, fill the insides, and cover with salt ; stand for two days, after which wipe dry with a cloth. Make a mixture composed of sixteen ounces of green ginger, salt and garlic (of each six ounces), two ounces each of red chillies and mustard seeds, and half an ounce of cardamons. Pound all these and fill the split mangoes with it. Boil for four minutes three large bottles of very good vinegar along with two pounds of sugar, one ounce of bruised ginger, and half an ounce of ground saffron. Stir till it comes to the boil. When cold pour over the mangoes, which you have put in glass bottles. When cold tie down.

WILPUSSAN CHAHKEE. (Curried Turnips.)

Young turnips are the nearest approach to Wilpussan that can be got in this country.

Put in a pot two pounds of small turnips cut in pieces ; add sufficient water to cover, also a teaspoonful of salt. Boil till quite tender, drain, and return to the pot, along with four ounces of ghee, two teaspoonfuls of Garam Massalla, a pounded red chilli, a pinch of saffron, and more salt if necessary. Stew for other twenty minutes, giving an occasional stir, so that all the spices are well mixed and the turnip in a soft mass. Eat with lentils, rice, ghee, new unleavened bread, chutnies, etc.

For European cookery turnips are simply boiled in salted water, drained, mashed, with pepper, salt, and butter added.

Mutter Chahkee. (Green Peas.)

Put in a pot of boiling water half an ounce of sugar and two pounds of shelled green peas, and boil steadily for twenty minutes; drain, and put them in another pot. Now fry lightly in four ounces of boiling ghee six ounces of roughly chopped onions, which add to the peas with a ground red chilli, and salt to taste. Stew gently for another twenty minutes. Eat with lentils, rice, new unleavened bread, ghee, chutnies, etc.

Dahl Falooree. (Spiced Lentil Crusts.)

Put into a basin two pounds of lentil flour which has been perfectly dried, two pounds of onions, a tablespoonful of parsley and sorrel (all finely chopped), a dessertspoonful of salt, and the same quantity of finely ground green ginger. Mix all thoroughly. Pour in sufficient water, very gradually, to make it into a paste which will stand by itself when dropped off a spoon. The mixture must be continually and smartly beaten when the water is being added so that it foams much like whipped cream. Boil eight slices of lemon peel in a deep pan half full of ghee. When the peel is thoroughly cooked take it out, and with a tablespoon drop the mixture in the shape of rocks into the boiling ghee, and allow to brown on all sides. Continue doing this till all the mixture is finished. Be careful to remove all floating particles before putting in additional mixture.

These must be eaten hot.

KARANJI. (Cocoanut Croquettes.)

Mix one pound coarse wheat flour, one ounce rice powder, four ounces ghee, and a little milk; knead, and roll out. Now mix half ounce rice powder and two ounces ghee. This is applied to the first, and the whole wrought together. Then the whole is made into small balls the size of a walnut and flattened with the hands into thin cakes.

Mix one and a half pounds grated cocoanut, four ounces poppy seeds, four ounces currants, half that quantity of cloves, and two pounds sugar. This is called "puran."

A little puran is put in the middle of each cake. They are then doubled over so as to enclose the puran, and the edges, after being wet, closely pressed, thus forming a purse shape. The cakes or croquettes are then cooked in boiling ghee.

SA-OO BHAHJEES. (Baked Apples.)

Peel and core as many apples as you require. Plug up the bottoms with pieces of other apples, and fill the centres with a mixture made of the following ingredients—viz., one ounce of the best ghee, two ounces of sugar, and one of lime-juice. Put rather more than an ounce of ghee in the bottom of a baking pan, on which lay the apples, sprinkle plenty of sugar on top, and cover the pan. Put them in the oven, and after ten minutes baste with their juice and a little more sugar; do this several times till three-parts done. Now add six ounces of lime-juice diluted to half its strength with water. Great care must be taken that the sugar and butter does not char. The liquid should be much of the same consistency and colour as dark golden syrup.

Shrikhand. (Sugared Cream.)

Reduce ten pounds of milk to a fourth of its bulk by boiling on a slow fire, so as to get a good thick cream, and put it into a towel and hang up to drip. When it is well drained take a chatty (deep dish or pan) and tie a rough towel over it. Then put a lump of the curd and a handful of sugar on the towel, and with the hand press the mixture through the towel into the chatty; continue doing this till all the curds are finished and three pounds of sugar used. Mix a thimbleful of saffron with a little milk, and add it along with a few ground cardamoms and some small pieces of broken sugar candy to the mixture.

Hulluah. (Cinnamon Sweet.)

Soak one pound of roughly ground wheat till the water is of a thickish milky nature. Strain this through a coarse cloth into a pan, in which you will also put half a pound of sugar. Boil till it begins to thicken (you must stir all the time); add six ounces of ghee in which you have boiled for five minutes six white cardamoms and six sticks of cinnamon. Continue stirring till mixture is thick. Remove seasonings; take pot from the fire, whip till it is like foam and make into large rough balls.

VII

CENTRAL PROVINCES (Mussulman)

MENU

Rohu-kā-Pillau (Pillau of Carp)	Māchi Hussānee (Trout Cutlets)
Keerā Chāhkee (Curried Cucumbers)	Chuckundā Chāhkee (Curried Beetroot)

Cofta-kā-Curree (Minced Kid Balls)	Kābutār Bhāhjee (Fried Pigeons)	Kullāh Yekhānee (Lamb Curry)
Goolgoolā (Cinnamon Balls)	Khir (Sugared Rice)	Rajah-ku-Pasand (Rajah Pudding)

Hulluāh
(Almond and Raisin Sweet)

ROHU-KA-PILLAU. (Pillau of Carp.)

Take two pounds of carp, free from skin and bones, and cut into two-inch squares. Cut four large onions into very fine slices, fry to a red brown in four ounces of boiling ghee, and place to the one side. Fry in the same ghee, for two minutes, one teaspoonful each of ground coriander and cumin seeds, half a teaspoonful each of cinnamon and cardamoms, a pounded point of garlic, a large red chilli ground to a powder, and a good pinch of saffron. Put in the pan the pieces of carp and brown very lightly on both sides.

Having soaked one pound of rice for a couple of hours, strain and put it into six ounces of boiling ghee and fry till all the ghee has been absorbed, after which place the fish on top, then the condiments along with the cooked ghee, a cupful of milk curd, a cupful of water, and a dessertspoonful of salt. Cover closely, and stew very slowly, taking care not to char. When the rice is quite soft put the whole mass on a dish, and strew the onions on top.

MACHI HUSSANEE. (Trout Cutlets.)

Remove skin and bones from two pounds of trout, mince very fine, and pound to a paste. Rub in half a teaspoonful each of ground white pepper, turmeric, ground onions, a large teaspoonful of salt, four tablespoonfuls of water, a cupful of rice flour, and two well-beaten eggs. When thoroughly mixed, take small portions and make into round balls, then with the hands flatten them out to the size of five-shilling pieces*and half an inch thick. String them on to iron or silver skewers, brush over with melted ghee, and roll in a plantain leaf (buttered paper will do). Grill in front of or over the fire. Eat with chapatee and fish chutney.

KEERA CHAHKEE. (Curried Cucumbers.)

Cut two pounds of cucumbers into inch lengths and steep in salt and water for two hours. Carefully drain as much of the moisture away as you possibly can, after which put them in a pot along with a teaspoonful each of ground onions, turmeric, coriander, and chillies, also four ounces of melted ghee and four of sliced onions which have been fried together, and stew gently till tender but not pulpy.

CHUCKUNDA. (Curried Beetroot.)

Boil two pounds of small roots till tender. When quite cold remove the skin very carefully; cut in slices and place in a pan with four ounces of melted ghee, a teaspoonful each of salt, turmeric, coriander, ground onions, and chillies, and half a cup of milk curd. Stew at the side of the fire for fifteen minutes. Eat with meats, vegetables, rice, and bread.

COFTA-KA-CURREE. (Minced Kid Balls.)

Mince and pound to a smooth paste two pounds of kid. Mix with this a large tablespoonful of strong broth made from the sinews and bones from the meat,

*The same size as half-dollars.

a tablespoonful of ground onions, a ground red chilli, a teaspoonful of salt, a cupful of ground rice flour, and two well-beaten eggs. Mix all this very thoroughly, and take small portions in the hands and form into balls rather larger than walnuts. In six ounces of boiling ghee fry two large onions finely shred, a teaspoonful each of ground turmeric and cumin, and half a teaspoonful each of caraway, aniseed, and red chillies. Now brown the balls; add half a cupful of the broth, the same quantity of cream (milk reduced to a fourth of its bulk by boiling), a pinch of red pepper, and a little more salt. Stew very slowly for at least two hours. Eat with rice or chapatee and chutnies.

KABUTAR BHAHJEE. (Fried Pigeons.)

Cut up six pigeons into halves. Stab the breasts and legs with a sharp knife. Rub them with a mixture of half a teaspoonful each of coriander and green ginger, a quarter-teaspoonful each of ground onions, cardamoms, cinnamon, and black pepper, and a good half teaspoonful of salt. Let them soak in this for an hour.

Fry in eight ounces of boiling ghee one pound of finely-sliced onions; when a red brown, place to the one side. Put into the ghee half a teaspoonful of ground red chillies and quarter of a teaspoonful of turmeric, and when boiling put in the pigeons (which you have wiped) and fry carefully on both sides, turning occasionally, so that the flesh may be thoroughly cooked. Dish with the onions strewn on the top, and eat with chapatee and chutney.

Lime Chutney.

Cut twenty-five limes into quarters half way through; stuff them with salt, and dry them for three days in the sun, bringing them in at sunset. Give them a good shake each time before putting them out in the morning. Mince small the dried limes. Pound in good vinegar twenty-five dry dates, fifteen large dry red chillies, three whole peeled garlics, and one ounce of green ginger. Mix all together and sweeten with sugar, first adding to it the strained juice of twenty-five limes. It will be ready in a week.

A cool oven will do in place of the sun.

Kullah Yekhanee. (Curried Lamb.)

Fry in eight ounces of boiling ghee four large onions finely sliced, and when red brown place to the one side. Now put in two pounds of fat lamb cut in inch-and-half squares, and fry lightly on both sides, first having sprinkled them with a teaspoonful and a half of salt. Put in the fried onions, a quarter of an ounce of cloves, a quarter of an ounce of ginger, a teaspoonful each of red chillies, turmeric, and coriander, six cardamoms, one ounce of sugar, two ounces of lime juice, two bay leaves, and one cupful each of water and milk curd. Cover very closely and simmer over a gentle fire for two hours. If the curry is too dry add a little more water; but there must be very little gravy. Eat with rice, chapatee, and chutney.

Tomato Chutney.

Bake in an oven two pounds of tomatoes until the skins burst; break them down, and mix with them a teaspoonful each of ground red chillies and salt, half a teaspoonful each of ground green ginger, ground onions, and mustard oil, a good pinch of sugar, and the juice of half a lemon.

Goolgoola. (Cinnamon Balls.)

In a pound of flour mix in a little yeast melted in one ounce of milk. Make a hole in the middle and add enough water to make a nice stiff dough; now work in one pound of sugar and fifteen ounces of milk, and place it on the fire in a pan along with six sticks of cinnamon. Stir the mixture till it becomes a soft, solid mass. When cool roll into small balls, and fry in plenty of boiling ghee.

Khir. (Sugared Rice.)

One pound of rice, two pounds of sugar, four ounces of blanched almonds, four ounces of sultana raisins, four ounces of sugar candy, two thimblefuls of ground cardamoms, and one thimbleful of saffron.

Wash the rice well, rub it with some ghee, and put in boiling water (double the quantity of rice). Boil till half-cooked, drain off the water, put it in a flat dish, and mix the saffron, the almonds (cut in halves), the raisins, and the sugar. Put a chatty (a deep pan or dish) on the fire, and pour in half a pound of the ghee; when boiling, put in the prepared rice and stir well till the sugar turns to a syrup. Cover it and simmer at the side of the fire till the rice has taken up all the moisture. Now put in the remaining ghee, the cardamoms, and the sugar-candy broken into small pieces; give it a stir, and remove from the fire. Before serving mix in a few pieces of pine-apple freed of skin and hard bits.

RAJAH-UL-PASAND. (Rajah Pudding.)

Ingredients.—Flour, four ounces; cream, four ounces (milk reduced to a fourth of its bulk by boiling); ghee, one pound; sugar, half a pound; ground almonds, four ounces; sliced almonds, two ounces; sultana raisins, two ounces; orange peel, one and a half ounces; six ground cloves; ground cardamoms, one dozen; nutmeg, one ounce; and half a dozen well-switched eggs.

Boil the sugar to a strong syrup. Stir in the flour gradually, and when boiling add the cream and melted ghee; stir well, then put in the fruits and mixed spices, and again bring to the boil. Remove the pan from the fire; stir in the switched eggs, beating all the time, and pour into a dish.

HULLUAH. (Almond and Raisin Sweet.)

Fry in a pound of boiling ghee one pound of roasted roughly-ground wheat, eight white cardamoms, and four sticks of cinnamon. Now stir in a pound of blanched and split almonds and a pound of sultana raisins, after which add a pound and a half of sugar syrup, and stir till it thickens. Pour on to an oiled deep flat dish, and when cooling cut into shapes; or it may be poured into oiled fancy forms.

VIII

CEYLON

MENU

Thora Malu
(Curried Mackerel)

Kellewelle Malu
(Curried Whiting)

Gona Malu Pirni
(Curried Elk)

Kukul Vejenjana
(Curried Fowl)

Kaytas
(Meat Balls)

Hava Malu Pirni
(Curried Hare)

Alle Vejenjana
(Potato Curry)

Labu Malu Pirni
(Curried Pumpkins)

Mulligatani
(Mulligatawny Soup)

Katta Bibick Kau
(Cocoanut Cake)

Alluwa
(Honey Cake)

Pala
(Fruit)

Cocoanut Chutney.

Six tablespoonfuls of scraped cocoanut, one red and three green chillies, half tablespoonful ground onions, the juice of half a lemon, and salt to taste. Grind all to a thin paste, and eat with curries.

Onion Chutney.

Moisten with cocoanut milk some roughly chopped onions and half the quantity of finely shred green chillies. Season with red pepper and salt and a very little lemon juice. Eat to curries.

Thora Malu. (Curried Mackerel.)

Fillet two medium-sized mackerels ; throw the heads, skin, and bones away. Rub the four pieces with a mixture of one and a half teaspoonfuls each of salt and ground onions, half a teaspoonful each of pounded cinnamon and chillies, and a quarter of a teaspoonful of pounded caraway and half the quantity of garlic, the juice of half a lemon, and a tablespoonful of mustard oil. Let the pieces of fish soak in this for two hours, turning them every fifteen minutes. Wipe each fillet, and cut in three pieces (twelve pieces in all), and plunge into plenty of boiling clarified butter, turning them once. When cooked they should be nicely browned on both sides. The fire should be a slow one.

Kellewelle Malu. (Curried Whiting.)

Take a few small onions, a teaspoonful of powdered "Bombay duck," half a teaspoonful ground chillies, a teaspoonful ground ginger, a point of garlic ground, the juice of a cocoanut, and half a teaspoonful of salt. Fry the onions sliced in a good bit of butter. When cooked, but not brown, add the chillies, ground ginger, garlic, Bombay duck, and salt; fry for a couple of minutes, then add a teacupful of thin cocoanut milk, and put in two pounds of whiting (without skin or bones) cut in two-inch pieces; cover up and cook for ten minutes in the oven, then add a cupful of thick cocoanut milk, and cook for other five minutes. When dished strew more powdered Bombay duck over the top.

Gona Malu Pirni. (Curried Elk.)

Wash two pounds of venison (in place of elk); cut it into small pieces, which put in a pan along with two teaspoonfuls of table salt, a point of garlic, four onions cut into slices, two inches ginger cut into slices, one teaspoonful coriander, and same quantity of turmeric; add two cupfuls of thick cocoanut milk, and place over a slow fire or in a cooking stove for two or three hours till the stuff is well but very slowly boiled. After boiling well, put into another pan, and put into the pan in which the meat was boiled a handful of onions cleaned and cut into thin slices. Add one tablespoonful clarified butter, and fry the onions over a slow fire; empty it into the pan in which the boiled meat was placed, and keep the pan over a slow fire for five or ten minutes. Before serving, however, and before the dish is brought to table, add three teaspoonfuls of lemon juice, and mix well.

Kukul Vejenjana. (Curried Fowl.)

Clean and cut into eight pieces a plump and tender fowl; fry in four ounces of boiling butter two middling-sized onions finely sliced. Place the onions to one side, and fry in the butter a teaspoonful each of turmeric and coriander powder, a quarter teaspoonful each of ground caraway seeds, cloves, sugar, one large red chilli, one large green chilli, and a teaspoonful of salt. Pour this and the fried onions into a pan, in which you have placed the fowl, with a teacupful of water and two tablespoonfuls of scraped cocoanut. After an hour's slow cooking add a breakfastcupful of thick cocoanut milk, and cook for another hour.

Kaytas. (Meat Balls.)

Chop up two pounds of any kind of raw meat, and pound very fine; season with cinnamon, caraway, pepper and salt. Add a little thick cocoanut milk and rice flour. Roll into balls and fry in plenty of clarified butter in which you have first fried a sliced onion. Add a very little broth and a touch of rice flour, sufficient to catch the gravy. Cook for a few minutes, till very little is left, Heat up the balls in this, and dish. Sprinkle some Garam Massala over them, and serve.

Hava Malu Pirni. (Curried Hare.)

Cut off the legs and shoulders, chop down the middle of the back, and then divide each side into two or three pieces, trimming away the ribs. Make a pint of gravy of the neck, head, liver, heart, ribs, etc., with onions, a good slice of beef chopped into small bits, a large carrot sliced, sweet herbs, and one dozen black peppercorns. Strain this into a stewpan and put the hare in. Now fry six shred onions in six ounces of butter till a light brown, which put in the pan. In the same butter put the following spices and condiments after being well mixed :—Half a teaspoonful of ground turmeric, the same quantity of ground coriander seeds, quarter of a teaspoonful each of ground cinnamon and ginger, twelve black peppercorns, six cloves, four cardamoms, and a point of garlic (all ground), and fry for three minutes, after which pour the whole into the pan with the hare, adding half a pound of good lean beef cut in small squares, a bunch of fine herbs, a bay leaf, the rind of a lemon, and one cupful of thick cocoanut milk. Add a teaspoonful of salt and a pinch of sugar. Cover the pan closely so that the steam may not escape. Set on a slow fire or in a slow oven for three hours. When done, skim the fat off the gravy; strain, and pour over the pieces of hare. There ought to be very little gravy.

LABU MALU PIRNI. (Curried Pumpkins.)

Remove the rind or the peel of two pounds of the fruit with a table knife ; cut into small pieces ; wash well in clean cold water ; put in a pan ; add a few onions cut into thin slices, some dry fish (Bombay ducks) ground into powder, half a teaspoonful each of turmeric, ground coriander, green ginger, and two green chillies cut into slices, half a teaspoonful of table salt, and two cupfuls of clean cold water; mix well, and place over a slow fire. Boil till the water evaporates. Add while being boiled a cupful of thick cocoanut milk and a spoonful of flour; keep stirring until the whole is well mixed up—for, say, five minutes. Remove pan from the fire, and let it cool a bit, and it will then be ready to be served at table.

ALLE VEJENJANA. (Potato Curry.)

Take one pound of potatoes, a few small red onions, one green chilli, half a teaspoonful of turmeric, a teaspoonful of salt, two teaspoonfuls of powdered Maldive fish or Bombay ducks. Boil the potatoes in their skins, and let stand till cold. Then peel and slice them. Slice the onion and chilli fine, mix a cupful of thin cocoanut milk with the potatoes and other ingredients, and stew very slowly for half an hour. When the gravy is well reduced add a teacupful of thick cocoanut milk and boil five minutes longer.

MULLIGATANI. (Mulligatawny Soup.)

Melt four ounces butter, and fry four sliced onions, and set to the one side. Fry in the same butter four teaspoonfuls of ground onions, one teaspoonful ground chillies, half teaspoonful ground ginger, and quarter teaspoonful ground garlic. Then fry a chicken, cut up into sixteen pieces, with two teaspoonfuls of salt, till browned.

Boil a spoonful of tamarinds in two breakfastcupfuls of stock, strain it, and mix with the fried chicken and condiments. Continue cooking for half an hour, then add half a quart of strong soup, putting in also the fried onions, a teaspoonful of flour, and a couple of bay leaves. Simmer at the side of the fire for a couple of hours, remove the bay leaves, and serve with boiled rice. When to be eaten European fashion increase the quart of soup to a gallon.

KATTA BIBICK KAU. (Cocoanut Cake.)

Take one measure rice flour and make it dry upon the fire ; grate three cocoanuts ; take one and a half bottles cocoanut honey and boil it well, and stir in the scraped cocoanut. After the cocoanut is well boiled with the honey take it from the fire and keep it for about fifteen minutes. After the interval mix it with flour, and some spice, and bake them like spongecake.

ALLUWA. (Honey Cake.)

Dry thoroughly in the oven some rice flour, and with cocoanut honey make a thinnish syrup. Boil well, then add more flour (just as you would do in making Scotch porridge), and boil till thickish, stirring all the time. Put into a flat dish, smooth the top, and when cold cut into neat pieces.

COCOANUT MILK.

Scrape the white of a middling-sized cocoanut, and pour over it two teacupfuls of boiling water. Squeeze the liquor out after it has stood for ten minutes. This is thick milk. To make the thin milk add other two teacupfuls of boiling water to the grated nut, and strain after fifteen minutes.

Cocoanut Honey.

Scrape a cocoanut and put it into a bowl ; pour half a pint of boiling water over it, and fifteen minutes afterwards squeeze all the liquor out. Then mix with this a quart of honey previously heated. When well mixed and cold put into a bottle for use.

IX

KASHMIR (Brahmin)

Menu

Svātch
(Wheaten Cakes)

Kāchaur
(Wheaten Cakes)

Bhātt
(Rice)

Dāl
(Lentils)

Hák
(Young Green Cabbage)

Sāg
(Lettuce)

Gogjū
(Turnip)

Kār
(Green Peas)

Cháman
(Sweet Cheese)

Hārriáh
(Milk Pudding)

Mo-Rubbā Phul-Pārouth
(Preserved Fruits and Wheaten Cakes)

Numāk Chā
(Salt Tea)

SVATCH. (Wheaten Cakes.)

These are made the same as Phulka. See Punjab (Brahmin) recipes.

KACHAUR. (Wheaten Cakes.)

These are made the same as Kachori. See Punjab (Mussulman) recipes.

PAROUTH. (Rich Wheaten Cakes.)

See Parantha in Punjab (Mussulman) recipes.

BHATT. (Rice.)

See Punjab recipes.

LENTILS.

See Punjab recipes.

HAK. (Young Green Cabbage.)

Take a large spring cabbage, break the leaves into pieces about the size of the hand ; steep in water. Put six ounces of oil in a pot and bring to the boil, in which place the pieces of cabbage, slightly shaking each piece before putting it into the pot. Cover closely, and cook till all the leaves are tender. Then remove to the side of the fire, and add a uarter teaspoonful of black pepper, one red chilli sliced, one teaspoonful of coriander, a teaspoonful of turmeric, and a teaspoonful of ginger. Give it a stir, and simmer till all the condiments are thoroughly amalgamated with the vegetable. If it is dry, add a little more water. Eat with rice and dal.

Sag. (Lettuce.)

Take two large tender lettuces, and break away the coarse part of the leaves. Steep in well-salted water, slightly shake the leaves, and put them in a pot with two ounces of oil. Cover closely, and cook till all the leaves are tender. Remove to the side of the fire, and add three ounces of oil, a quarter teaspoonful of black pepper, one ground red chilli, one teaspoonful each of coriander, turmeric, and green ginger, and a sliced green chilli. Stir well, and add a little more oil if necessary. Place on the fire and simmer till all the condiments are thoroughly amalgamated with the vegetable. Eat with rice, dal, cakes, and chutnies.

Gogju. (Turnip.)

Clean your turnip and cut into pieces about an inch square, which place in a pot with a little water, and boil till nearly tender; drain, and add a sliced red chilli, two sliced green chillies, salt, a teaspoonful of coriander, a teaspoonful of cumin, and three ounces of oil, and cook till perfectly tender but not pulpy. Eat with rice, dal, cakes, and chutnies.

Kar. (Green Peas.)

Clean one pound of green peas, and place in a pot with boiling oil and a little water; boil till nearly tender, then add half a sliced red chilli, two green chillies sliced, salt, and half a point of garlic, and cook till perfectly tender but not pulpy. Eat with rice, dal, cakes, and chutnies.

CHAMAN. (Cheese.)

Boil some oil in a pan; put in six slices of firm cream cheese a quarter of an inch thick, and fry quickly on both sides. Make a strong syrup of sugar and water, and when boiling pour over the pieces of cheese, and keep hot till the cheese is thoroughly saturated with the syrup. Serve in a dish and eat warm.

This may be eaten with boiled rice, leaving out the sugar.

HARRIAH. (Milk Pudding.)

Two ounces sugar, four and a half dwts. ground almonds, two ounces milk, two and a half dwts. nishashta, one half ounce ghee. Bring the ghee to boiling point, and fry the nishashta in this. Make the sugar into a strong syrup, add the milk, ground almonds, and syrup, and when the nishashta is well cooked and thick remove from the fire.

NISHASHTA.

Put some whole wheat meal flour in a pot with plenty of water, and boil for half an hour. Strain through a cloth into a dish, expose to the air for some hours, and when solid it is ready for use.

NUMAK CHA. (Salt Tea.)

See Mussulman recipe.

Apple Jelly.

Wash apples, and remove any decayed parts. (Crab apples are the best.) Put them in a preserving pan and cover with water ; boil till perfectly soft. Strain through a jelly bag, and to every pound of juice add a pound of sugar, and boil briskly for seven or eight minutes. Skim carefully, and pour into jars while hot, and cover when cold.

Apple Jam.

Put the apples on the fire again with more water, and after boiling for half an hour pass all through a sieve, and put to it the juice of a lemon to every three pounds of pulp, and three quarter pounds of sugar to each pound of pulp, and boil for half an hour.

Apple Cheese.

Proceed as above, only put the pots in a cool oven till all the moisture has evaporated.

Orange Marmalade.

Cut twenty-four Seville bitter oranges in two. Squeeze the juice out, and scrape away the pulp, rejecting all pith and pips. Boil the skins in water till quite tender, and cut into very fine chips after having removed all the pith. Take the same weight of sugar as the oranges, and clarify it ; add the chips, pulp, and juice, and boil for ten minutes ; now add the juice and grate of four lemons, and boil for twenty minutes, skimming carefully, and stirring occasionally in case of burning.

X

KASHMIR (Mussulman)

MENU

Kalach
(Wheat Meal Scones)

Bhătt
(Rice)

Dāl
(Lentils)

Kābāk
(Quails)

Gosfānd
(Lamb)

Ahū
(Venison)

Khobáni
(Sweet Mutton Cutlets)

Khír
(Rice and Milk)

Halvā Sohan
(Saffron Cakes)

Mo-Rubbā Phul-Pārouth
(Preserved Fruits and Rich Wheaten Cake)

Numāk Chā
(Salt Tea)

Kalach. (Wheat Meal Scones.)

Prepare a nice dough with four pounds of rough wheat meal, two ounces of butter, a little salt, and three ounces of German yeast, and sufficient water so that you can handle it; add more water if too thick, and more meal if too thin. Put it in a deep can, and keep in a warmish place for an hour to rise; then knead it well. Form into round balls, clap them flat with the hands, and make a hole in the middle; slip on to sheets of iron, and set for another hour to rise; then bake in a good oven.

Kabak. (Quails.)

Take six quails, remove the heads, tails, and legs, then cut them in two. Put one pound of oil in a pot and bring to the boil; in this put two large finely shred onions; cook till red; then place to the one side. In the same oil brown the pieces of quails on both sides, then put in a cupful of water and a cupful of curd, the onions, one teaspoonful of salt, a shred red chilli, a teaspoonful of cinnamon, a teaspoonful of coriander, a pinch of saffron, a teaspoonful of cardamoms, and three or four pieces of green ginger. Cover closely, bringing all to the boil; then simmer gently until the quails are cooked. Add more water if necessary, and keep them from charring.

Gosfand. (Lamb.)

Take two pounds of lamb cut in two-inch pieces. Put half a pound of oil in a pot, and bring to the boil.

In this put two large finely shred onions, and cook till red; place to the one side. In the same oil brown the pieces of lamb on both sides, put in two cupfuls of water, the onions, one teaspoonful of salt, half of a shred red chilli, a teaspoonful of cinnamon, a teaspoonful of coriander, one or two pieces of green ginger, and half a dozen cardamoms. Cover closely, bringing all to the boil, then simmer gently until the meat is cooked; add more water if necessary, and be careful to keep the meat from charring.

AHU. (Venison.)

Take two pounds of lean venison, cut in two-inch pieces, and wash thoroughly. Put half a pound of oil in a pot, and bring to the boil; in this put two large finely shred onions, and cook till red, then place to the one side. In the same oil brown the pieces of venison on both sides, put in a cupful of water and a cupful of curd, the onions, one teaspoonful of salt, a shred red chilli, a teaspoonful of cinnamon, a teaspoonful of coriander, a teaspoonful of sugar, half a teaspoonful of cloves, the juice of a lemon, three or four pieces of green ginger, and two preserved quinces cut in quarters. Cover closely, bringing all to the boil, then simmer gently until the meat is cooked. Add more water if necessary, and be careful to keep the meat from charring.

KHOBANI. (Sweet Mutton Cutlets.)

Mince two pounds lean meat very fine, in which mix sufficient oil to make it stick together, one teaspoonful of ground cinnamon and one ounce of ground almonds; and when well mixed make into round tabloids about the size of a two-shilling piece* and a quarter of an inch thick. Place a sultana raisin in the middle of each. Bring strong sugar syrup to the boil, in which put these rounds one by one, and boil till each round is thoroughly saturated with the syrup. Take them out of the syrup and put them in a pan of boiling oil, and fry on both sides till cooked. Place them on a dish, mix the syrup and oil, and bring to the boil, stirring all the time; pour it over the tabloids.

Khir. (Sweet Rice.)

Wash, dry, and thoroughly grind one pound of rice, and put on the fire in milk. Boil till quite thick. Sweeten well with sugar, and stir in a good flavouring of rose water.

Halva Sohan. (Saffron Cakes.)

Take three ounces of ground rice, two pounds six ounces of milk, one pound three ounces of sugar, two ounces of ghee, two and a half dwts.† of pistachios, and a little saffron.

Mix the milk with the rice, and put it in a pot on a light fire, and keep stirring till it becomes granular and the milk is absorbed. Then put in the sugar which you have made into a syrup, boil till nearly candy high, put in the ghee, stir for a little, and remove from the fire. Put in sufficient saffron to give a good flavour, and beat

*The same size as a quarter.
†One tablespoon (more may be used if desired).

well till it is light and creamy. It should be soft but firm. Form into small balls, and with the hands flatten them to about the size of half-a-crown.* Sprinkle the pistachios, which you have chopped, on top of each tabloid.

PRESERVED MULBERRIES.

Make a pint of juice by boiling sufficient berries for the purpose. Strain it through a jelly bag, and put it in a pot with two and a half pounds of sugar; boil up, skimming carefully; then add two pounds of ripe mulberries. When heated put the pot on the fire, and simmer very gently till the berries are nearly soft. Put them in an earthenware crock for twenty-four hours. Boil again very gently, and, when the fruit is soft, but not broken, and the syrup jellies when tested on a cold plate, pour into pots and tie down when cold.

PRESERVED GRAPES.

Proceed in the same way, using a third less sugar. They require a much longer time to cook, and do not require such gentle handling as the mulberries.

QUINCE PRESERVE.

Put in a pan with sufficient water to cover them, four pounds of good ripe quinces which you have peeled, cut in quarters, and cored. Boil till tender, then put them on a rough sieve for an hour or so to drain. Now put them into a preserving pan, in which you have the

*The same size as a half-dollar.

same weight of sugar boiled to nearly candy height. Boil, and when the liquor jellies quickly when tested (by dropping some on a cold plate) it is finished. Pour into pots, and twenty-four hours afterwards tie down.

QUINCE JAM.

Proceed in the same way as you did for Preserve; only, after you have drained them, you pass the pieces through a fine sieve before putting into the boiling sugar.

NUMAK CHA. (Salt Tea.)

Take tea according to the number of people present, put it into water well seasoned with salt, bring it to the boil, then pour it out and serve with hot milk. No sugar.

XI

MADRAS (Hindu)

MENU

Ānnām
(Rice)

Pāppu
(Lentils)

Neyee
(Clarified Butter)

Birungi Sukhadas
(Curried Artichokes)

Anti Kâya Pulusu
(Green Banana Curry)

Vuralāgeddā Kurā
(Curried Potatoes)

Mirāpā Chāru
(Mulligatawny Soup)

Ānnām Perugu
(Rice and Curds)

Pûri
(Semolina Biscuits)

Bâdam a Hālvā
(Almond Pudding)

Kobbara Rotahlu
(Cocoanut Pancakes)

Bâdum a Drâksha
(Nut and Raisin Sweet)

Rojâpoovu Mittâyee
(Rose Tablet)

Pumdlu
(Fresh Fruits)

Annam (Rice).

Cook the same as in Mysore Hindu recipe.

Pappu. (Fried Spiced Lentils.)

Wash and pick half a pound of lentils; when thoroughly dry, roast the same as you would do coffee beans.* Now put into a pan three teaspoonfuls of ground onions, one teaspoonful of ground large red chillies, half a teaspoonful turmeric, half a teaspoonful ground green ginger, a quarter teaspoonful ground garlic, one and a half teaspoonfuls of salt, then the lentils, and pour in sufficient water till it stands two inches above the mixture. Give it a good stir, put it on the fire till the lentils are all dissolved, being careful not to disturb the contents till they are cooked into a soft solid mass. Now take and whisk the mass with a wire whisker (in lieu of a churn) till quite light. Cut a pound of onions in slices, not too thin, and fry till a reddish brown in two ounces of boiling ghee. Heat four ounces of ghee in a pan, chop up the onions, which, along with the lentils, put into the ghee, and simmer at the side of the fire for twenty minutes.

Birungi Sukhadas. (Curried Artichokes.)†

Wash one pound of rice, and drain. Fry in boiling ghee or melted butter five ounces sliced onions; when a nice brown add one teaspoonful each of cinnamon and cardamoms, one red and six green chillies, a quarter teaspoonful of cloves, one garlic point, and a teaspoonful

*To roast, place on a pan in a 400° oven for about ten minutes.
†Curried Jerusalem Artichokes.

of salt, and fry for five minutes. Then add the rice, and fry till very little browned.

Take two pounds of Jerusalem artichokes, peel and cut them into inch and a half pieces, and steep in cold water for half an hour. Take half a pound of Bengal gram (lentils or yellow peas will do), wash and boil till soft, and add the artichokes to it with a pinch of cayenne pepper and a tablespoonful and a half of tamarind juce, and allow to simmer very slowly.

In a separate pan put a few sliced onions, sliced green ginger, and a pinch of mustard seeds ; fry all these in boiling ghee till the onions are nicely browned. Now put altogether in a close pot along with a cup of milk curd and another of water, the rice, and a teaspoonful of saffron ; simmer till the whole is like a porridge. Now put in the artichokes, which should be soft but not pulpy ; if they are inclined to get too soft, take them out. Add salt to taste. Eat with other vegetables, chapatee, ghee, chutnies, or pickled fruits.

ANTI KAYA PULUSU. (Green Banana Curry.)

Wash and scrape the skins of two pounds of green bananas, cut them in square pieces about one and a half inches long ; take an ounce of tamarind juice, two teaspoonfuls chilli powder, one teaspoonful of coriander powder, and one teaspoonful turmeric powder, and mix together and ground to a paste ; add salt to taste. Slice two big onions ; add two bay, two lemon grass, and two coriander leaves, and some water. In a separate pan fry the two onions, a point of garlic, and a pinch of mustard seed till they are brown, and put into the main dish. Close the lid and allow to simmer till the vegetables are cooked. Add two spoonfuls of melted butter.

Eat with other vegetables, rice, ghee, lentils, pickled fruits, or chutnies.

VURLAGEDDA KURA. (Curried Potatoes.)

Clean two pounds of potatoes, cut in quarters, boil a cupful of lentils till they are quite soft, and put them all together ; add the juice of two ounces of tamarinds (which you get by pouring a small teacupful of boiling water over them), two teaspoonfuls of red chilli powder, and salt to taste.

In a separate pan fry a tablespoonful of minced onions, one teaspoonful of minced green ginger, a couple of teaspoonfuls of coriander, a teaspoonful of turmeric, a spoonful of mustard seed, and half a spoonful of caraway seeds. After these are fried in the boiling ghee, place the whole amongst the potatoes and lentils till the consistency is like very thick soup. The potatoes, however, are not to be too soft.

Eat with other vegetables, or separately with rice, lentils, ghee, or chutnies.

RADISH CHUTNEY.

Clean and cut the roots in pieces as large as a big bean. Make a sauce of a ground red chilli, a pinch each of ground poppy seeds, ground coriander, and cumin, the juice of one lemon, a tablespoonful of thick milk curd, and a little salt.

MIRAPA CHARU (Rice and Mulligatawny).

Make the same as in Mysore Hindu recipe.

FRUIT PICKLE.

Wash and dry equal quantities of dates, prunes, and dried apples (cored and peeled). Stew the dates for ten or twelve minutes, and cut them into rings, throwing away the stones. Cut the apples into quarters and the prunes in halves, throwing away the stones. Now put the fruits in wide-mouthed jars in layers, sprinkling over each finely sliced ginger, peppercorns, and sticks of cinnamon, and a little salt. Make a syrup of a quart of wine vinegar and one pound of sugar, and pour over the fruits, which must be well covered. Cork very tight and expose to the sun for some days, and lay to the one side for a couple of months.

PICKLED PLUMS.

Take any kind of plums not quite ripe, peel, and put them in salt, and expose to the sun for a couple of days. Now shake them free of water, and put a layer into bottles, over which put green chillies, cloves of garlic, finely sliced green ginger, and peppercorns, and continue this till the bottle is full, finishing off with a little salt. Be sparing of the garlic. Fill the bottle with good wine vinegar, close tightly, and put out to the sun every day for a month.

ANNAM PERUGU. (Rice and Curds.)

Boil the rice in the usual manner, and mix with it a good quantity of curdled milk.

Curdled Milk.

Bring the milk to blood heat, and put a small piece of rancid ghee or a few drops of lemon juice in, and stand to the one side till milk thickens. Strain the liquid off and you have the curd.

Puri. (Semolina Biscuits.)

Mix two pounds and a half of semolina with four tablespoonfuls of melted ghee and a pound and a half of sugar ; mix well together, then pour in gradually ten ounces of milk, and last of all as much flour as will make a good dough ; let it be well kneaded, and then allowed to stand for two or three hours. Take portions of the dough and shape them like biscuits, and fry in boiling ghee till they acquire a rich brown colour.

Badam a Halva. (Almond Pudding.)

Dissolve sugar in water and boil it to a thick syrup. Soak some rough ground wheat for twenty-four hours, and pound it well ; squeeze the milk out of the pulp and add it to the boiling syrup, and keep stirring. Then pour in gradually some melted ghee, stirring all the time, after which add a good quantity of ground almonds, and when well mixed pour the whole into a plate, and squeeze out the superfluous ghee. Eat with puri.

This can be preserved for a fortnight or more.

The soaked grain is useless.

Malpua. (Cocoanut Pancakes.)

Make a paste with water or milk of one pound of granulous flour of wheat, three ounces of butter, and two ounces of rice flour ; knead it well. Roll out in about twenty-four very thin pancakes of the size of a cheese plate. The thinner they are the better.

Roast or bake separately one pound castor sugar, half pound ground cocoanut, and quarter ounce ground cardamoms till they get red brown in colour.

Take one pancake and spread over it some of the baked castor sugar, cocoanut, and cardamoms ; put another pancake upon it, spread again, and continue till you have made one pancake of four, then fry it in boiling ghee. Six pancakes are thus made.

BADAM, PHUL MITHAI. (Pistachio, Almond, and Raisin Tablet.)

Boil two pounds of sugar and three ounces of ghee in a pound of water to crackling height.

Meanwhile, having reduced three pounds of milk to a fourth of its bulk by boiling, remove the boiled sugar from the fire, stir in the milk along with five ounces each of chopped pistachios, almonds, and sultana raisins ; keep stirring till thick and creamy ; colour slightly with the juice of spinach ; then pour out into oiled forms, or a deep dish, in which case you would cut it into lengths when nearly cold.

ROJAPOOVU MITTAYEE. (Rose Tablet.)

Proceed exactly the same as in Lemon Tablet, only substituting attar of roses and carmine colour for lemon essence and saffron colour.

XII

MADRAS (Mussulman)

Menu

Khābab Māchli
(Grilled Salmon)

Māchleekā Sālān
(Curried Soles)

Gosh-Kā-Pillau
(Pillau of Mutton)

Khābôbs
(Meat Rissoles)

Murgika Sâlan
(Curried Chicken)

Châval aur Khārgosh-Ka-Sālān
(Rice and Curried Hare)

Dum-Kā-Rout
(Imperial Pudding)

Muzāffer
(Saffron Toast)

Nāsh Pātee
(Baked Pears)

Akhrote-Ka-Mithai
(Almond Tablet)

Phāl
(Fresh Fruits)

KHABAB MACHLI. (Grilled Salmon.)

Cut eight fillets into two-inch squares and wash thoroughly in cold water. Make a mixture of one teaspoonful each of ground coriander, turmeric, red chillies, and salt, a pinch of mace, a ground point of garlic, and a tablespoonful of tamarind juice. Rub the pieces of salmon with this, and let soak for an hour. Now wipe the pieces and thread them on to skewers with a piece of pickled mango between each fillet. Roast in front or over the fire.

MACHLEEKA SALAN. (Curried Soles.)

Remove the heads, tails, and black skin from two soles each weighing about a pound. Cut each into three pieces and wash thoroughly. Rub well with the following mixture—one teaspoonful each of turmeric and coriander, half a teaspoonful each of ground garlic, red chillies, and salt. Lay to the one side for an hour. Fry in four ounces of boiling ghee four ounces of finely shred onions, and when nicely browned place to the one side. Wipe the pieces of fish, and fry them lightly on both sides. Now put in the fried onions and add a tablespoonful of water and one of cream (milk reduced to a fourth of its bulk by boiling), two ounces ghee, four inches cinnamon, a large red chilli sliced, three cloves, a ground point of garlic, a pinch of saffron and a little more salt. Close the lid of the pot very tight, and stew very slowly at the side of the fire for half an hour. Eat with bread and fish chutnies. There should be little or no gravy.

GOSH-KA-PILLAU. (Pillau of Mutton.)

Take a big, wide-mouthed vessel with a tight lid, and fry in half a pound of boiling ghee one pound small onions sliced, five sliced green chillies, quarter ounce whole cloves, half ounce whole cardamoms, quarter ounce stick of cinnamon, and fry till the onions are a brown colour. Cut two pounds of mutton in small pieces, which place in the pan with condiments, and continue frying, stirring from time to time; add one cupful of milk, one cupful of curds, and salt to taste; boil till the meat is almost cooked, then add a paste made of quarter ounce of garlic, half ounce green ginger, half ounce poppy seeds, one ounce almonds, and the juice of one lemon.

In another vessel boil one pound of rice along with a little salt, and six cloves, twelve cardamoms, and a stick of cinnamon. When the rice is half boiled, strain it, picking out the cloves, &c. Spread the rice evenly over the cooked meat in the first vessel, and on which sprinkle melted ghee and saffron water. Close the lid. Keep the vessel over a gentle fire, and put some live coals over the lid, or put it in an oven till the rice is fully cooked. Before dishing mix the rice and meat.

KHABOBS. (Meat Rissoles.)

Mince two pounds of mutton or beef very fine, and mix thoroughly with it a teaspoonful of ground onions; add a pinch of cayenne pepper, a teaspoonful of powdered coriander, same quantity of turmeric, a pinch of powdered cloves, and salt to taste.

Take iron rods about the thickness of a pencil and a foot long, rub them with ghee and coat them with the paste about one inch thick, winding a sewing thread round in a spiral fashion to keep the meat from falling off. Place these in front of the fire, turning often, or put them in the oven till they get brown. Remove the thread, slip the rods out, and cut in pieces. Serve with the pillau.

MARGIKA-SALAN. (Curried Chicken.)

Fry in four ounces of boiling ghee four sliced medium-sized onions; then fry three teaspoonfuls of ground onions, one teaspoonful of ground turmeric, one sliced red chilli, a teaspoonful of whole ginger, a teaspoonful of poppy seeds, a teaspoonful of roasted coriander seeds, and a quarter of a teaspoonful of ground garlic. When brown lay in the chicken (which you have cut in eight parts), and fry to a nice brown, then add one teaspoonful and a half of salt with a cupful of water, also curdled milk till gravy is thick, and simmer very slowly for at least an hour. Serve with rice, ghee, and pickles.

KHARGOSH-KA-SALAN. (Curried Hare.)

Remove the legs, and cut the back into three pieces, and place the seven pieces in water. Boil four ounces of ghee, in which fry two large onions sliced, one teaspoonful coriander, turmeric, cumin, poppy seeds, mustard seeds, and cardamoms, a broken stick of cinnamon, one point of garlic, three coriander leaves, one bay leaf, an inch of green ginger, and a teaspoonful of salt. When the onions are browned, fry the pieces of hare in the above till brown all over, then pour into the pot a cupful of water, a cupful of cocoanut milk, and two cupfuls of curds. Cover the pot very close, and bring to the boil. If too little liquid, add some more curds. A few minutes before serving, stir in a teaspoonful of sugar and two tablespoonfuls of tamarind juice. Serve with rice, ghee, and pickles.

TAMARIND JUICE.

Pour a pint of boiling water over four ounces of tamarinds, and twenty minutes afterwards squeeze and strain.

DUM-KA-ROUT. (Imperial Pudding.)

Take half pound of flour, one and a half pounds of ghee, one pound of sugar, three ounces of almonds blanched and sliced, six ounces of walnuts, three ounces of dried figs (both chopped), half pound of cream (milk reduced to a fourth of its bulk by boiling), quarter ounce of cloves, half ounce of cinnamon, quarter ounce of cardamoms (all three ground), and quarter ounce of yeast.

Melt the yeast with a little milk, add it to the flour with the rest of the cream, and mix lightly.

Beat the sugar and ghee to a cream, then add it along with the fruits and spices to the flour, and mix all together lightly. Set in a warm place for two hours to rise, after which put on an oiled broad pan and apply heat to top and botton, or place in the oven.

MUZAFFER. (Saffron Toast.)

Put six thick slices of bread toasted very crisp into a pan, and pour over half a pound of melted butter.

In another vessel boil for fifteen minutes three glasses of milk, half a pound of sugar, a quarter pound of ground almonds, and half a teaspoonful of saffron. Pour this into the first vessel, and boil the whole for a few minutes till it gets to a thick porridge. Pour it into a dish, and when cold serve with cream.

NASH PATEE. (Baked Pears.)

Peel, cut in halves and scoop out the cores of six large pears. Fill the hollows with a mixture made up of one ounce of the best ghee, two ounces of sugar, and one of lemon juice, adding a clove in each. Put an ounce of ghee in a deepish baking tin, and place the halved pears on it, and sprinkle some sugar on top of them. Cover the pan, and after ten minutes baste with their juice and more sugar. Baste every now and then till three parts done. Now pour into the pan six ounces of lime-juice diluted to half its strength with water, and finish cooking. Great care must be taken that the syrup does not char. It should be of a thickish consistency, and brownish in colour.

Akhrote-Ka-Mithai. (Almond Tablet.)

Mix two pounds of sugar and four ounces of ghee in a pound of water, and boil to crackling height.

Having reduced three pounds of milk to a fourth of its bulk by boiling, remove the sugar from the fire and stir in the milk along with a pound of cleaned and finely-chopped almonds. Stir till thick and creamy, and pour into any kind of oiled dish fancy may dictate.

Walnut Tablet.

This is made the same way, substituting walnuts for almonds.

XIII

MYSORE (Hindu)

MENU

Annāh (Rice)

Byālleh (Lentils)

Tuppā (Clarified Butter)

Vānghee Bāth
(Pillau of Egg-Plant)

Moolāngi Geddeh Hūlli
(Horse-raddish Pods)

Seemeh Moolāngi na Pālyā
(Stuffed Carrots)

Annāh
(Rice)

Menāsinā Chāru
(Mulligatawny Soup)

Annāh-Māssāru
(Rice and Curds)

Hālvā
(Pudding)

Lāddu Moti Choor
(Flour Croquettes)

Chiver
(Sugar Crusts)

Nunbe Hannina Mittai
(Lemon Tablet)

Hānnu
(Fresh Fruits)

ANNAH. (Rice.)

Wash rice thoroughly and steep for half an hour; plunge it into furiously boiling water, stirring lightly to keep the grains separate. When nearly soft, drain and return to the pot to dry, stirring occasionally to keep it from adhering. Serve in a large bowl.

BYALLEH. (Boiled Lentils.)

Wash and boil the lentils, drain off the water (keep it), and return lentils to the pot. They should be thoroughly boiled—not too pulpy, but much of the same consistency as boiled rice. Serve in a large bowl.

VANGHEE BATH. (Pillau of Egg-Plant.)

Take one pound of egg-plants which wash, divide each into four, and fry in boiling ghee, remove the portions and place to the one side. Wash one pound of rice, dry it, then fry in the same ghee.

In a separate pan fry the following in ghee:—Five ounces sliced onions and four garlic points, half ounce stick of cinnamon, half ounce of cloves, three ounces of cardamoms, half ounce cinnamon leaves. Then put the fried condiments amongst the rice, and add sufficient water to more than cover the rice. Boil all this till the rice is three-quarters done, and then add the fried egg-plant to it, with two cupfuls of cocoanut milk, six or seven green chillies pounded to a paste, six ounces skinned almonds, three ounces rosewater, a pounded red chilli, and a pinch of saffron (just enough to colour);

stir this all up and add eight ounces of ghee. Cover closely and bring to the boil, and place to the one side so that it may simmer steadily and gently for three quarters of an hour till the rice is completely cooked. Add enough salt to taste.

MOOLANGI GEDDEH HULLI. (Horse-radish Pods.)

Take two pounds of the long pods which grow on the horse-radish tree. Wash and cut into lengths of about two inches. Fry in four ounces of ghee one pound of finely shred onions, then fry the pods lightly, and put in a teaspoonful of ground coriander and cumin seeds, half a teaspoonful each of ground ginger and red chillies, a teaspoonful of salt, half a cupful of water, and a cupful of curd. Stew till tender.

CUCUMBER CHUTNEY.

Peel and take out the seeds of a cucumber and grate it. Mince two green chillies, half ounce green ginger, half teaspoonful of whole mustard seeds, half the quantity of cardamom seeds; mix with the cucumber, then add half a teaspoonful salt, a tablespoonful sour milk, the juice of a lemon, and three ground coriander seeds. Mix all together thoroughly, and serve after three or four hours.

MOOLANGI NA PALYA. (Stuffed Carrots.)

Clean some carrots and cut them into two-and-a-half inch lengths, then cut little pieces off the ends of each length, and fry the whole in ghee. When fried, scoop out the centre of the carrots, leaving one end closed, and fill them with the following mixture:—One ounce each of chopped almonds and pistachio nuts (first skinning the nuts), a little grated carrot, a saltspoonful of salt, and a tablespoonful of Garam Masala, first binding the stuffing with some melted butter and a very little rice flour. Fry in boiling ghee or butter.

ANNAH MENASINA CHARU. (Rice and Mulligatawny Soup.)

Take two tumblerfuls of the water in which the lentils were boiled, and to it add half an ounce of tamarind juice, four garlic points, two large onions cut in quarters, half teaspoonful turmeric, ten whole black peppercorns, four red chillies, and salt to taste, and allow the whole to boil.

In a separate pan bring to boiling point some ghee, add a pinch of mustard seeds, a pinch of caraway seeds, two bay leaves, and two lemon leaves, and after frying them for four or five minutes add to the stock along with twelve green coriander leaves. Bring to the boil, and simmer at the side of the fire for half an hour. When dishing take out the various leaves and condiments. It should be rather a clear soup, and is thickened with boiled rice. Served from the large bowl.

ANNAH-MASSARU. (Rice and Curds.)

Boil the quantity of rice required in the usual manner. Boil double the weight of milk to a thick curd (less than a fourth its original bulk) and mix with the boiled rice.

HALVA. (Pudding.)

Fine wheaten flour (half a pound), quarter pound of ghee, half a pound of sugar, and a pint of water. A dessert-spoonful of powdered almonds, same of cocoanut, and a tablespoonful of sultana raisins and pistachio nuts.

Put the butter in a hot pot ; let it steam slightly. Put in the flour, and keep stirring till it turns slightly brown. The whole of the ghee will be taken up by the flour at this stage. The sugar, having already been turned into a carefully skimmed syrup in the above water, is now put in with the almonds, cocoanut, pistachio nuts, and raisins. A lot of steam will now rise with a good deal of frizzling sound, then everything quietens down. Do not put the lid on. Keep stirring very carefully with a spoon to prevent it from sticking to the bottom of the pan, but do not shake. The water will evaporate in about a quarter of an hour. The flour will go on collecting into a mass, and the ghee will begin to separate to a certain extent when the free water has all evaporated. Then not only stir the mass with a spoon, but also lift a part of it with the spoon till it will easily slip from it. The consistence will be that of a solid soft mass. Dish hot and dust with powdered almonds and cocoanut, and serve with cream.

LADDU MOTI CHOOA. (Flour Croquettes.)

Soak overnight some white peas, and when soft pound smoothly and pass through a sieve. Put into a cloth and very thoroughly press all the moisture out. When dry put into a pan with a little ghee and sufficient milk curd so that when cooked it will be a fine soft mass. Add more ghee and cook again. Be sure to stir all the time. It should now be a soft mass easily handled, but not sticky. Take small portions and roll into balls, first putting some sultana raisins and chopped almonds into them. Boil sugar to a thready degree, place the balls in it and bring to the boil, remove from the fire, and after half an hour's soaking put the balls on a drainer, and when quite dry they are ready to be served.

CHIVER. (Sugar Crusts.)

Rub a little ghee into one pound of very fine flour, and knead it well. Cover and put a weight on top of it, After an hour put a lump in a basin and beat into a foam, and continue doing this till the dough is finished. Put a deep pan on the fire half filled with ghee, and when boiling pour half a cupful of the paste in very slowly, raising your hand whilst doing so. Turn it once, and when cooked remove with a skimmer and dip it into four pounds of sugar, which you boiled to nearly candy height. When nicely coated remove to the one side, and continue till the paste is finished.

NUNBE HANNINA MITTAI, (Lemon Tablet.)

Boil two pounds of sugar and three ounces of ghee in a pound of water to crackling height.

Have ready two pounds of milk reduced to a fourth of its bulk by boiling. Remove the sugar from the fire, and stir in the milk along with some essence of lemon and a little liquid saffron to give a good yellow colour. Stir till all is thick and creamy, pour into oiled shapes or into a dish an inch deep, and when nearly cold cut into lengths about an inch broad.

VANILLA TABLET.

Made exactly as above, only substituting essence of vanilla for essence of lemon.

XIV

MYSORE (Mussulman)

Menu

Māchleekā-Sālān (Curried Salmon)

Bhunihui Māchli (Fried Soles)

Khābuthārka Pillau
(Pillau of Pigeons)

Gāyekā Kurmā aur Chāvāl
(Curried Beef and Rice)

Bāttākh-Kā-Kurmā
(Stewed Goose)

Jillebee (Macaroni Sweet)

Kheer (Sweet Rice)

Kāddu Hālvā (Vegetable Marrow Sweet)

Phāl
(Fruit)

MACHLEEKA SALAN. (Curried Salmon.)

Cut two pounds of salmon into slices one inch thick: wash thoroughly. Rub well with the following mixture; One teaspoonful each of ground turmeric, coriander, red chillies, and salt. Lay to the one side for an hour. Fry in four ounces of boiling ghee four ounces finely-shred onions; when nicely browned place to the one side. Wipe the pieces of fish and fry them lightly on both sides. Now replace the fried onions, and add a tablespoonful of tamarind juice, two tablespoonfuls of water, four ounces of ghee, four inches cinnamon, a large red chilli sliced, a point of garlic, a pinch of saffron, a bay leaf, two coriander leaves, three cardamoms, and a little more salt. Stew very slowly at the side of the fire for half an hour. There should be little or no gravy, but be careful not to char. Remove the condiments, &c., and eat with bread and fish chutnies.

BHUNIHUI MACHLI. (Fried Soles).

Take two soles weighing about one pound each, remove the heads, tails, and black skin, and cut in three pieces; wash thoroughly in cold water. Make a mixture of one teaspoonful of coriander, turmeric, and ground onions, half a teaspoonful each of red chillies and salt, a pinch of nutmeg and mace. Rub the pieces of sole with this and leave for an hour. Boil four ounces of ghee, and fry four ounces of finely-shred onions to a nice brown and place to the one side; then place the fish in and fry on both sides till thoroughly cooked, on a slow fire.

Strew the onions on top, and eat with bread and fish chutnies.

KHABUTHARKA PILLAU. (Pillau of Pigeons.)

Clean three pigeons, and cut each into three pieces; wash them in salted water in which you have placed some ground turmeric. Fry in boiling ghee half a dozen small sliced onions, a point of garlic, a large red chilli sliced, three sliced green chillies, half a dozen cloves, same quantity of cardamoms, and a piece of cinnamon. When the onions are brown, dry and fry the pieces of pigeons. Keep moving so that they may not char. Now add a cupful of water, a cupful of thick curds, and salt to taste. Bring to the boil, and simmer very gently for half an hour. Five minutes before the meat is tender, add half an ounce of green ginger, a teaspoonful of poppy seeds, same quantity of coriander, and an ounce of almonds pounded into a paste, mixed with the juice of a lemon. Stir well.

In another vessel boil half a pound of rice (which has been well washed) along with a little salt, three cloves, six cardamoms, half-inch stick of cinnamon, and a little saffron. When the rice is half cooked, strain it, picking out the cloves, cardamoms, and cinnamon. Spread the rice over the meat in the first vessel, pour melted ghee on top, cover, and cook till the rice is tender.

GAYEKA KHURMA AUR CHAVAL. (Curried Beef and Rice.)

Fry in boiling ghee two large onions sliced very fine, six sliced green chillies, one large red chilli sliced, half a teaspoonful of mustard seeds, quarter of a teaspoonful of caraway seeds, a teaspoonful of cumin seeds, a teaspoonful of coriander seeds, a teaspoonful of poppy seeds, a point of garlic, and a teaspoonful of salt. Pound all to a paste before frying.

Fry two pounds of beef cut in small pieces till browned, then add the condiment paste with a cupful of water, a cupful of thick curd, and a tablespoonful of tamarind juice. Close the lid, and stew very slowly for an hour. Serve with plain boiled rice, and any Indian pickled vegetables such as chutnies, cucumbers, &c. Leavened bread may also be eaten.

BATTAKH-KA-KURMA. (Stewed Goose.)

Clean a young goose about seven or eight pounds in weight. Cut it into sixteen pieces; wash and dry them. Rub with a mixture of salt, pounded cumin, cardamoms, cinnamon, and white pepper, and let stand for an hour.

Fry in eight ounces of boiling ghee four large onions sliced, a paste made of one teaspoonful of coriander, one teaspoonful of turmeric, one teaspoonful of cumin seeds, one teaspoonful of mustard seeds, a teaspoonful of poppy seeds, half a teaspoonful of caraway seeds, half a teaspoonful garlic, six large sliced green chillies, one large red chilli sliced, a stick of cinnamon broken in pieces, and a little lemon juice. When the onions are browned, add the pieces of goose, which fry lightly. Pour into the pot two cupfuls of cocoanut milk, two cupfuls of thick curd, and two cupfuls of water. Stir all together, then add a couple of bay leaves, six coriander leaves, a handful of sultana raisins, and a dozen of almonds blanched and cut in halves. Cover, and stew gently for three hours. Ten minutes before dishing put in the juice of a lemon. Remove the leaves and the rougher pieces of the bird, and serve with rice, bread, and pickled vegetables.

JILLEBEE. (Macaroni Sweet.)

One pound wheat flour, one pound ghee, one and a half pounds rice flour, one ounce gram (or pea) flour, one ounce lentil flour, and one ounce and a half of milk curd.

Mix the flours and curd with an ounce of ghee into a paste, and keep over-night. In the morning put it into a large dish and beat it into a foam. If too thick, sprinkle some milk over it so as to make it sticky. Put a pan on a slow fire, and pour the ghee in it. Make a strong syrup of the sugar beforehand, and keep it near you. Then take a tin cup and make a hole in the bottom as large as a pea, hold it over the boiling ghee, and pour the paste into the cup, having your left hand finger on the hole. Then remove your finger and make four rounds in the boiling ghee as many times as the frying pan will hold, turn them with a skimmer, and remove as dry as possible, and put them into the syrup. Place to the one side, and repeat the process till all the paste is finished.

KHEER. (Sweet Rice.)

Take half a pound of rice, wash it well, and steep for an hour. Then boil till soft, but not pulpy. Pour over half a pound of strong sugar syrup in which you have boiled two sticks of cinnamon and six cardamoms. Remove the cinnamon and cardamoms, and just before dishing stir in a large cupful of cream.

KADDU HALVA. (Vegetable Marrow Sweet.)

Take two pounds vegetable marrow, one and a half pounds ghee or butter, half pound sugar, two ounces rosewater, and a pinch of saffron.

Having cleaned the marrow, cut it into small chunks, and let them boil in water for about thirty-five minutes. When the marrow is well boiled, drain off the water into a basin (keep this water). Put the marrow in one and a half pounds of boiling butter, and let it cook for half an hour, taking care that you do not burn it. In the meantime put the sugar into the water that was drained from the marrow, and put on to the fire and boil till it becomes thick. After which pour it over the pieces of marrow, and keep it on the fire till all the water has evaporated. Just before taking it off the fire put the rosewater and a touch of saffron in it. To be eaten hot.

XV

NEPAL

Menu

Motichur
(Fruit Liquor)

Bhāt (Boiled Rice)	Dāl (Lentils)
Mānsu Pakuwā (Boiled Meats)	Mānsu Bhutura (Fried Meats)

Tihun
(Stewed Meats)

Achāri Thāri-Thāri Ko (Various Chutnies)	Māchhā Ko-Achār (Fish Chutnies)

Dāhi
(Curdled Milk)

Dūdh
(Plain Milk)

Māsālā
(Dried Fruits)

MOTICHUR. **(Fruit Liquor.)**

Ferment any kind of fruits; concentrate, and load with strong spirit. Syrups of all kinds can be bought, which may be boiled and the spirit added along with different kinds of spices.

BHAT. (Boiled Rice.)

Wash rice, and drain. Put some water into an earthenware pot, which place on the fire. When the water is boiling plunge the rice in, and when the water is evaporated the rice is ready.

DAL. (Lentils.)

Wash some lentils and steep overnight. Put them in a pot with some of the water they were steeped in, also a tablespoonful of pounded onions, a teaspoonful each of ground coriander and cumin seeds, a pinch of red pepper, and a little salt. When thoroughly cooked there should be very little moisture. Finish by pouring a good quantity of cooked butter or ghee over.

MANSU PAKUWA. (Boiled Meats.)

Cut two pounds of beef, veal, mutton, lamb, pork, kid, or venison, well mixed with fat, into nice pieces, and boil in three cupfuls of water till tender. A quarter of an hour before finished add a cupful of thick curd, a teaspoonful each of coriander (pounded), red chillies, and salt, and a good pinch of nutmeg, and twenty-four small mushrooms. Bring to the boil and simmer till tender and very little moisture. Eat with rice, bread, ghee, and chutney, and serve with other dishes.

MANSU BHUTURA. (Fried Meats.)

Cut two pounds of beef, veal, mutton, lamb, kid, pork, or venison into thin slices of about three inches long. Smear them with a mixture composed of a teaspoonful each of turmeric, coriander, ground onions, red chillies, a point of garlic, and half a teaspoonful of salt. Let the meat soak for an hour, slightly shake the pieces, and fry on both sides in plenty of boiling ghee.

Chickens, pheasants, partridges, guinea-fowls, and pigeons may be cut in pieces and cooked the same way.

TIHUN. (Stewed Meats.)

Cut a cleaned duck into eight pieces, and fry them in boiling ghee or butter in which you have first browned a finely chopped onion. Put the whole in a pot with three cupfuls of water, and of turmeric, coriander, and poppy seeds a teaspoonful, of caraway and cumin seeds half a teaspoonful, a pinch of assafœtida, half a teaspoonful of salt, and a quarter of a salt-spoonful of red pepper. Bring to the boil and stew slowly for an hour. Now put in eight potatoes cleaned and cut in quarters, one large carrot cut in two-inch pieces, and some broad beans or haricot beans which have been softened by soaking. Stew slowly for another hour, or till the meat and vegetables are very tender. A few minutes before dishing add two cups of milk curd and a little warm water, as there must be plenty of gravy. Eat with rice, lentils, and chutnies.

Mutton, lamb, veal, beef, kid, pork, venison, chickens, pheasants, partridges, guinea-fowls, rabbits, hares, and pigeons may be cooked as above.

DAHI. (Curdled Milk.)

Heat some milk in a pan (but do not boil it), put in a small piece of rancid butter about the size of a pea, cover up and keep in a warm place till the milk has thickened, which will be in about eight hours. You can prepare it as given in Asia Minor or Punjab Mussulman recipes. For sweet curd you boil milk till it is a fourth of its original bulk. Served with meats.

Plain milk is now served, after which all dishes are removed, and tobacco and preserved fruits partaken of.

XVI

PARSEE (Festival)

MENU

Chevāl Vagaralle
(Fried Rice)

Tuverni Dāl Masallāh
(Spiced Lentils)

Tarāii Mechli
(Fried Fish)

Yarali Ida
(Fried Eggs)

Iestu
(Stewed Vegetables)

Pilauh Māchilimo Sas
(Fish Balls and Sauce)

Samosā
(Pancakes)

Kustār Kārkārien
(Custards and Almonds)

Korharāno Murembo
(Pumpkin Preserve)

CHEVAL VAGARALLE. (Fried Rice.)

TUVERNI DAL MASALLAH. (Spiced Lentils.)

Both of these dishes are prepared the same way as given in the " ordinary " Parsee dinner.

TARAII MECHLI. (Fried Fish.)

Take two teaspoonfuls of ground onions, one teaspoonful of large red chillies, two teaspoonfuls of salt, half a teaspoonful of poppy seeds, and half the quantity of aniseed. Grind all these into a fine powder and smear on both sides eight fillets of sole (two soles), and put to the one side for two hours. Fry a nice brown in sufficient boiling ghee to cover them, and eat with bread and chutnies.

YARALI IDA. (Fried Eggs.)

Fry in boiling ghee two sliced onions. When light brown put them to the one side, and fry six eggs on both sides, sprinkling top and bottoms with a mixture of half a teaspoonful of turmeric, half a teaspoonful of coriander, quarter of a teaspoonful of ginger, a quarter of a teaspoonful of red large chillies, and a teaspoonful of salt, all ground and carefully mixed. Trim off the ragged edges, and eat with bread, &c.

IESTU. (Stewed Vegetables.)

Put in a pot three parsnips, one tender carrot, three potatoes, and half a pound of shelled green peas. Cut the potatoes in eight pieces, and the other ingredients accordingly.

Fry in boiling ghee or butter two sliced onions, and when browned put to the one side, and fry the following, viz. :—Half a teaspoonful of coriander, salt, and mustard seeds, a pinch each of aniseed and poppy seeds, and a suspicion of garlic, all ground before frying. Put in the vegetables (cut in pieces), a cupful of water, the same of milk curd, and two ounces of ghee, and stew till tender. Eat with bread.

PILAUH MACHILIMO SAS. (Fish Balls and Sauce.)

Pass two pounds of fish (raw or cooked), free of skin and bones, through a sieve. Put in a few breadcrumbs, of each a teaspoon of fine herbs, coriander, and cumin seeds, half the quantity of aniseed and red chilli, all ground together and fried in ghee, in which you have first fried a couple of sliced onions. Remove the fried onions, and mix the fish with the condiments, a dessert-spoonful of salt, and an egg, and make into balls about twice the size of walnuts.

Take the fried onions and put in a pan with more boiling butter, heat up and place to the one side, and fry three pounded coriander leaves, one green chilli, a teaspoonful of ground green ginger, quarter of a tea-spoonful of garlic, and a teaspoonful of salt. Grind all together and fry in the boiling butter. Now fry the fish balls till cooked, and put in the centre of a dish and surround with boiled rice, and pour the following sauce on top of the balls.

Soles, haddocks, whitings, cod, halibut, turbot, perch, or hake may be cooked the same way.

Sweet Sour Sauce.

Cook half a teaspoonful of flour in four ounces of vinegar and four dessert-spoonfuls of sugar. When the flour is cooked remove the pan to the side of the fire, and stir in four eggs whipped with a little water. See that the sauce does not boil. Eat with bread.

Samosa. (Pancakes.)

Soak eight ounces of rice overnight, grind it to a pulp, mix in four ounces of flour, adding two ounces of ground almonds and a little rosewater. Whip in four whole eggs and sufficient sugar to sweeten. Reduce the whole to a rather thin consistency with milk, and fry portions in butter rather thicker than European pancakes.

Kustar Karkarien. (Custard with Almonds.)

Blanch and pound four ounces of sweet almonds with a little rosewater. Stir a teaspoonful cornflour into half a pint of milk, then add the pounded almonds and sufficient sugar to sweeten. Whip six eggs with a little water and add to the foregoing, mixing well. Put the mixture in a pot on a very low fire, and stir till it has thickened. Be careful not to boil, or eggs will curdle. Put in glasses and serve with sweetened rice wafers.

Korharano Murembo. (Pumpkin Preserve.)

Pare and core a pumpkin, cut in pieces and hang in a cool place till all the moisture is away. Take one pound of the pulp and one pound sugar, mix thoroughly, and put on fire; when sugar is melted put in three drams of wheaten starch melted in water, and when it is thick put into a dish which is smeared with butter. Make level with top of dish and cut into small squares. Strew the top with ground cardamoms and almonds.

XVII

PARSEE (Ordinary)

MENU

Cheval Vagāralle
(Fried Rice)

Tuverni Dal Masāllah
(Spiced Lentils)

Khimnā Kābāb
(Mince Meat Balls)

Kāchubār
(Salad)

Ramās Kātlās
(Salmon Cutlets)

Tarāloo Gose Anā Vatanā
(Fried Meat with Green Peas or Beans)

Vagāralle Mārga
(Roast Fowl)

Mālida
(Wheat Flour Pudding)

Murenboo Aninās No
(Preserved Pine-apple)

CHEVAL VAGARALLE. (Fried Rice.)

One pound rice, four cloves, seven cardamoms, one teaspoonful each of caraway, black pepper, and aniseed, two onions, and a quarter of a pound of ghee.

Slice the onions very fine, and fry in ghee to a dark-brown colour, but do not char ; then put in all the condiments, and fry for three minutes, now put in the rice, after washing it thoroughly, along with two pounds of water and three drams of salt. Boil till all the water has evaporated, and place it at the side of the fire to dry.

Take a quarter of a pound of blanched and split almonds, a quarter of a pound of cleaned and plumped currants, and half an onion sliced fine, and fry along with the almonds and currants in ghee. Dish the rice and strew these on top. Serve with lentils, meat balls, and salad.

TUVERNI DAL MASALLAH. (Spiced Lentils.)

Take one pound lentils, two teaspoonfuls salt, two teaspoonfuls of turmeric, one pound onions, half pound vegetable marrow, handful of coriander leaves, two and a half teaspoonfuls of green ginger, and half a pound cleaned potatoes.

Thoroughly wash the lentils. Put them into two pounds of water, along with the salt, turmeric, onions cut in quarters, vegetable marrow, leaves of coriander, ginger, and potatoes cut in quarters. Mix them all up, then put in two large sliced red chillies, one and a half drams caraway seeds, a teaspoonful each of cinnamon and cardamoms, and three drams of pepper, all dried and pounded. Put all this with the lentils and another pound of water. Bring to the boil, then place the pot at the side of the fire to simmer till all the moisture has nearly evaporated and the mixture is of the consistency of thinnish porridge. Fry a point of garlic in butter and mix it along with the lentils. Serve with fried rice, meat balls, and salad.

KHIMNA KABAB. (Mince Meat Balls.)

One pound of finely-minced meat, quarter of a pound of onions, a handful of coriander leaves, two large ground red chillies, two teaspoonfuls of cinnamon, two teaspoonfuls of ground poppy seeds, one of ground ginger, a point of garlic, three ground cloves, six ground cardamoms, two whole eggs, and one teaspoonful of salt.

Slice the onions and fry in ghee till they are slightly browned; put them to the one side and fry the various seasonings for a couple of minutes, and when cool mix in the meat along with the salt, a little milk curd, a teaspoonful of flour, and the eggs; stir well in a bowl, and then take small portions in the hands and form into balls rather larger than walnuts, and fry in plenty of boiling ghee. Of course the coriander leaves are kept out. Eat with fried rice, lentils, and salad.

KACHUBAR. (Salad.)

Take three onions, cut them in very thin slices, and lay them in some salt for half an hour. Drain carefully, and put in minced coriander leaves, two sliced red chillies, a suspicion of garlic, a little minced green ginger, two sliced tomatoes, and a shred lettuce. Pour in a tablespoonful of spiced vinegar, and mix all thoroughly together, and serve with rice, lentils, and meat balls.

Ramas Katlas. (Salmon Cutlets.)

Take three slices of a small salmon about an inch thick, rub with salt, and lay aside for half an hour. Then remove all the skin and bones. Grind a teaspoonful of coriander seeds, half a green chilli, and some red pepper and salt. Smear the pieces of fish with this and lay to the one side for an hour; afterwards egg and breadcrumb them, and fry in boiling ghee. Eat with bread.

Taraloo Gose Ana Vatana. (Fried Meat with Green Peas or Beans.)

Take one pound of meat, one pound and a quarter of ghee, one pound and a quarter of onions, one teaspoonful of ground green ginger, two handfuls of coriander leaves (two teaspoonfuls of ground coriander seeds will do instead), one teaspoonful of turmeric, half a teaspoonful of garlic, three green chillies, three quarters of a teaspoonful of salt, half a saltspoonful of red pepper, one pound of shelled green peas, and a quarter pound of water.

Cut in thin slices one quarter of a pound of the onions, and fry in the ghee along with the ginger and garlic, till they are a light brown; then put in the meat cut in inch squares, and fry till browned all over. Pour in the water, and a quarter of a teaspoonful of salt, and stew very slowly for an hour and a half. Half an hour before the meat is cooked put in the green peas, the pound of onions thickly sliced, the green chillies sliced, the turmeric, the pepper, and the rest of the salt, also the coriander leaves. Serve with bread.

Vagaralle Marga. (Roast Fowl.)

Take a good plump chicken, one and a half pounds of ghee, six large potatoes, four large green chillies, a saltspoonful of pepper, and a teaspoonful of salt.

Put the chicken into a pan with the ghee, and fry it. After it is browned all over, take out the ghee, leaving a small quantity in the pan. Put in half a pound of water with the chicken, the six potatoes cut in halves, the chillies sliced, the salt, and pepper. Stew very slowly till the bird is very tender. Eat with the potatoes and bread or rice.

Malida. (Wheat Flour Pudding.)

Take three quarters of a pound of coarse wheat flour, two ounces of fine white flour, seven eggs, half a pound of ghee, one and a half pounds of sugar, half a pound of almonds, two ounces of rosewater, half a teaspoonful of powdered cardamoms, and rather more than half of that quantity of nutmeg.

Mix the two flours with the eggs, six ounces of the ghee, and half a pound of milk. Make dough of this, and roll into balls about the size of small lemons. Fry these in the other two ounces ot ghee. When cooked, put them in a dish and bruise into a soft mass and mix with the syrup of sugar; pass through a sieve, return to the pot, and put in the almonds (which have been blanched and fried in ghee), the rosewater, cardamoms, and nutmeg. Stir over the fire till thoroughly cooked, and of the consistency of thin porridge.

MURENBOO ANINAS NO. (Preserved Pine-apple.)

Boil half a pound of the pulp of a pine-apple with the same weight of very heavy sugar syrup for a quarter of an hour. Eat when cold.

XVIII

PUNJAB (Brahmin)

Menu

Puri
(Wheaten Cakes)

Kạrāh
(Turkish Delight)

Tarkári-Ka-Pullah
(Pillau of Vegetables)

Alu Meyání Pur
(Stuffed Potatoes)

Pálāk
(Spinach)

Kaddu
(Vegetable Marrow)

Khumb
(Mushroom)

Khíchadí né Kadhí
(Curdled Rice and Curd)

Dál
(Lentils)

Ghee
(Clarified Butter)

Chaval
(Rice)

Phulka Massoor
(Pistachio Pastry)

Bhāt Pullau
(Rice Pillau)

Am Kustel
(Mango Fool)

Rasgulláh
(Milk Croquettes)

Perạ
(Rose Tablet)

Phirní
(Rice and Nut Sweets)

Gūlāb Jámin
(Pine-apple Sweets)

PURI. (Wheaten Cakes.)

Mix water and flour, and knead it till it is a well-mixed dough, soft, but easily handled. Small portions of this dough is then taken and beaten between the hands into thin flat cakes about five inches in diameter. Cook in boiling butter and eat with karah.

Karah is made very much the same as Turkish delight.

KARAH. (Turkish Delight.)

Soak one ounce of gelatine in a cupful of water; boil very fast for four minutes two pounds of pure cane sugar in a cupful of water and the juice of two lemons, being careful to remove any scum. Take the pan off the fire and put in a little cochineal colouring and essence of rose. Pour the boiling sugar over the gelatine, stir till all is thoroughly mixed and quite smooth. Pour it into oiled dishes about an inch deep, and when cold cut into shapes and cover with fine powdered sugar.

TARKARI-KA-PULLAH. (Pillau of Vegetables.)

Fry in boiling ghee two pounds of sliced onions and three sliced green mangoes (which have been stoned and steeped for several hours) till nicely browned—place them to the one side. Wash four ounces of rice and fry in three ounces of boiling ghee; when beginning to take colour, and all the ghee absorbed, remove from the fire.

Take two pounds of any kind of vegetables in season, cut them up and put in a pot with very little water, a pinch of garlic, a teaspoonful each of salt, turmeric, coriander, cumin, cloves, cinnamon, all unground, and a slice red chilli ; cook till tender. Now add the rice along with three ounces of ghee. Give all a stir round, close the pot very carefully, and simmer at the side of the fire till the rice is quite tender. When the pillau is cooking, if there is not enough of moisture, add some more water or a little milk curd. Dish and strew the fried onions and mangoes on top. Eat with lentils, chutnies, etc.

GHEE. (Clarified Butter.)

This is prepared as follows :—Milk is slowly boiled in large earthenware pots for a couple of hours. It is then left to cool, a little curdled milk called dhye being stirred into it to induce coagulation. In time the contents of the jars are transferred to a large earthenware crock, in which they are patiently worked with a piece of split bamboo. After about half-an-hour's careful working, hot water is thrown over the mass, and in the course of another half-hour or so, the churning being continued, the butter forms. This butter is then left until it is rancid. It is then put into an earthenware vessel and boiled until all the water is evaporated, and mixed up with a little salt or betel-leaf, and bottled for future use.

ALU MEYANI PUR. (Stuffed Potatoes.)

Cut little pieces off the ends of cleaned potatoes and fry the whole in melted butter till cooked. Take an ounce each of skinned and chopped almonds and pistachio nuts; but first make a seasoning of half teaspoonful of salt, a pinch of pepper, half a teaspoonful of ground red chillies (large), a quarter of a teaspoonful of ground garlic, two teaspoonfuls of ground onions, and four teaspoonfuls of garam masalla. When pounded together and well mixed, put in a little curdled milk and some melted butter or ghee. Hollow out the potatoes and fill with this mixture. Then join the separate pieces with a batter made of flour, melted butter, and curdled milk, and again fry in ghee.

GARAM MASALLA.

Is made thus:—Grind and mix together four ounces of cumin seeds, half an ounce of cloves, half an ounce of cinnamon, half an ounce of small cardamoms, and half an ounce of large ones.

PALAK. (Spinach.)

Wash well a pound of spinach leaves. Put them in a pan with a teaspoonful of turmeric, half the quantity each of caraway and salt. Steam till cooked, then add four ounces of ghee or melted butter, and cook for a little longer till all the moisture has nearly evaporated.

KADDU. (Vegetable Marrow.)

Steam four ounces of butter or ghee, then put a large onion cut into dice into a stewpan, and one tablespoonful of Garam Masalla, a teaspoonful of green ginger, a teaspoonful of coriander, and a point of crushed garlic; keep them stirred over a moderate fire, but do not brown them. Then add a pint of water, let it just boil up; put in the pieces of vegetable marrow cleaned, cut into inch and a half squares, which stir round two or three times to mix with the condiments, and put the stewpan over a slow fire or in a warm oven for half an hour; when done (which you may ascertain by pressing a piece between finger and thumb; if done, it will be quite tender), add the juice of a lemon and a tablespoonful of curds and a little salt; stir the whole round two or three times gently to mix, and turn out upon your dish. Serve with phulka, rice, and chutnies.

Phulka.

Knead some wheaten flour with water, put in some salt, let it stand for twenty minutes, after which take small pieces, of which make small balls; then with the hands beat then into very thin cakes, and cook both sides on a flat piece of iron which you have standing a little above the fire.

Khumb. (Mushrooms.)

Clean and skin a pound of mushrooms and cut into small pieces. Heat three ounces of ghee or melted butter, and fry a little pepper, salt, and half a teaspoonful of turmeric for two minutes, then place in the chopped mushrooms. Cover closely and cook slowly for half an hour.

Khichadi ne Kadhi. (Curried Rice and Curried Curd.)

These are two separate dishes, served together at dinner. Khichadi is a curried preparation of rice and split lentils or split peas, and kadhi is a curried preparation of curd in the manner herewith described.

Khichadi. (Curried Rice.)

To one pound of rice add a quarter pound of split lentils or split peas; wash them well, and put them on the fire to boil, with just the amount of water as would form a layer of about one inch over them, till half cooked. Mix in a frying pan containing some boiling ghee half a pound of ground cocoanut, an eighth ounce each of cloves, cumin, whole black pepper, Mesua Terrea or chestnut flour, cardamoms, cinnamon, assafoetida, a quarter ounce each of ground turmeric and coriander; fry them till they assume a dark brown colour, then stir them well into the half-cooked rice and lentils, with one ounce of salt and one eighth ounce of ground black cardamoms. Boil the whole till dry. If the rice and lentils are not well cooked (which can be ascertained by pressing some of them between fingers), add some hot water, and again boil to dryness. Eat with kadhi.

Kadhi. (Curried Curd.)

Switch one pound of very sour curd, and add one and a half pounds water. Switch again thoroughly. Add one ounce gram flour and put the mixture to boil on the fire. Keep on stirring. After it boils once, add an eighth ounce of assafoetida, two ounces of ghee or butter, one ounce of salt, a quarter ounce of powdered turmeric. Boil for ten minutes. It is better to have it in the form of a thin paste; and eat with khichadi.

Dal. (Lentils.)

One breakfastcupful of lentils soaked for two hours in warm water, after which wash in cold water. Four breakfastcupfuls of water, two teaspoonfuls of salt, a pinch of ground cloves, one tablespoonful of Garam Masalla, one tablespoonful of butter or ghee, and half an onion. Put the lentils in watér along with the salt and cloves, and let it boil on a slow fire till quite soft and semi-fluid in consistence, with lentil seeds swelled and floating in thick fluid on top, though partly broken down. Then take another pot and steam the butter in it, put in the sliced half onion, the curry and Garam Masalla, till brown, then put in the lentils along with a tablespoonful of the curds of milk. Remove from the fire and serve.

Bhat. (Rice.)

Wash rice, and put in a pot with water standing two inches over it; boil briskly till all the water is evaporated. Shake it up, and again put on fire or in the oven to dry. Give it an occasional shake to separate grains.

Phulka Massoor. (Pistachio Pastry.)

Work one pound of gram flour and one pound of ghee into a paste that will roll out. Make a strong syrup of one pound of sugar and half a pound of water. Roll the paste out into a sheet a quarter of an inch thick, and cut into rounds of about three inches in diameter, and score them rather deeply crossways with a knife; cover with syrup; bake in an oven till the syrup is well soaked in and the rounds quite brown. Before getting cold cover with sliced pistachios.

Bhat Pullau. (Sweet Rice Pillau.)

Take one pound of rice, one pound of sugar, eighth of an ounce of cardamoms, five ounces of melted ghee or butter, two ounces of almonds, two ounces of pistachios, and two ounces of sultana raisins.

Wash the rice in three waters, and then soak for half an hour. Put three and a-half pounds of water in a pot, and, when boiling, put the rice in and boil quickly till half cooked. Strain the rice on a sieve, giving it a stir to separate the grains. Put one third of the melted ghee into a pot, and when it begins to boil put in the cardamoms, which have been soaked in water for half an hour. Boil eight ounces of water with one pound of sugar for two or three minutes, then put in the half-boiled rice, and mix well. Put on the lid till it boils, then remove the lid and stir until all the water has evaporated. Add the almonds, pistachios, and raisins, cover the pot with the lid or a cloth, and steam for half an hour. Pour the contents into a dish and sprinkle the rest of the melted ghee or butter over it, also adding two ounces of strong perfumed water.

Am Kustel. (Mango Fool.)

Remove the skin and stones from six green mangoes, cut them in quarters, and steep for several hours in cold water. Drain carefully, and put in clean cold water and boil till quite tender, then pass them through a sieve. Put them into another pan, sweeten to taste, and add very gradually (stirring all the time) as much rich milk as will reduce the pulp to the consistency of a good custard. A few grains of white cardamoms may be added along with the sugar.

Rasgullah. (Milk Croquettes.)

Six tumblers of milk, lemons sufficient in number.

Boil the milk, and squeeze the lemons in till milk curdles. Pour the mass into a muslin bag, and hang it up till all the water is away. Then make it up into small balls, with an almond and a few cardamom seeds in the centre of each. Roll the balls in flour—just enough to keep the particles together. Fry these in ghee or butter till brown, then put them in syrup for a day, and serve.

Pera. (Rose Tablet.)

Take a pound of milk, the same quantity of sugar, and boil them candy high. Remove the pan from the fire, stir in a few drops of cochineal and attar of roses, and beat till all is thick and creamy. Pour on to an oiled dish, and when nearly cold cut into small round cakes about an inch and a half in diameter.

GULAB JANIM. (Pine-apple Sweets.)

One pound of flour, one pound and a half of sugar and five or six drops of kewra or essence of pine-apple. Mix the flower well with a quarter pound of ghee, then put in sufficient water to make a good dough. Make small balls the size of a walunt, and fiatten them, and fry in ghee. Boil the sugar till near crackling degree, remove from the fire, and put in the flattened balls, and let remain for half an hour, and put on oiled paper to dry.

PHIRNI. (Rice and Nut Sweets.)

Boil two pounds six ounces of milk, and stir in one ounce rice flour slowly, so that the flour is mixed completely with the milk. When it is reduced to six ounces remove it from the fire, and mix in four ounces of sugar, one ounce almonds (already ground), one ounce of pistachio nuts, and one ounce of raisins ; or cut them into pieces and then mix them up. Afterwards put the phirni in a plate and spread some silver and gold leaves over it.

XIX

PUNJAB (Mussulman)

Menu

Máhí Palao
(Fish Pillau)

Pātaur ni Pāpetā
(Fried Potatoes)

Bhāji
(Vegetable Curry)

Biriāni
(Fried Chicken)

Kābāb-i-Títer
(Roasted Partridges)

Kormá
(Curried Mutton)

Paláō
(Pillau of Kid)

Bitē Kelia
(Baked Banana and Cocoanut)

Motichoor Lāddoo
(Spiced Sugar Balls)

Zārdá
(Sweet Rice)

Rábbrí
(Curdled Milk and Fruit)

Phirnī
(Rice Sweet)

Amrití
(Vanilla Tablet)

Bálúshái
(Orange Tablet)

MAHI PALAO. (Fish Pillau.)

Take two pounds white fish, one pound rice, nine ounces ghee, one pound goat's flesh, and fifteen grains each of cinnamon, cardamoms, and cloves, half a pound of onions, seventy-five grains black pepper, three ounces curd, and half ounce salt.

Cut the fish into pieces about two inches long and one broad, and steep in plenty of lemon juice. Cut the onions in fine slices and fry in half of the ghee. When nicely browned, place to the one side, and fry the condiments for two minutes, then brown the fish on both sides. In a separate pot boil one pound goat's flesh in plenty of water till all the good is taken out of it, remove the meat, and put into the stock two pounds of rice. When the moisture is evaporated, and the rice tender, dish it; put the pieces of fish on top, then the condiments, and finish by pouring the rest of the ghee over, which has first been boiled for two or three minutes. Eat with bread and chutnies.

PATAUR NI PAPETA. (Fried Potatoes.)

Take some large potatoes and have them peeled and cleaned. Cut square pieces out of them, and have them fried in butter. When this is done, take some flour and put some salt as well as red and black pepper in it, and mix it with coagulated milk or curds (dahi), with which coat the pieces of potato and again have them fried, after which the pataur will be done. The milk may be curdled with rennet.

BHAJI. (Vegetable Curry.)

One pound of shelled peas, four under-boiled skinned potatoes, each cut up into four pieces, two tablespoonfuls of ghee, half a teaspoonful of salt, a teaspoonful of curry powder, three cupfuls of water, and half of a small onion.

The salt, curry powder, and onion are to be pounded up into a paste. Fry these in slightly steaming ghee or butter for a minute; avoid charring. Put in the potatoes and peas, and keep stirring them until the potatoes are quite brown. Do not let them burn. Then put in the water and let it steam for half an hour. The peas and potatoes should be of such a consistence that they can be quite easily pressed between finger and thumb. Serve with boiled rice and chutnies.

The curry powder to be made as follows :—

CURRY POWDER.

Two ounces turmeric, one ounce coriander seeds, one ounce cumin seeds, half ounce each yellow mustard and caraway seeds, one ounce poppy seeds, quarter ounce cloves, half ounce mace, one ounce each of large and small cardamoms, half ounce garlic, one ounce green ginger, one ounce cinnamon, one ounce large red chillies. Dry thoroughly, and pound till it will pass through a fine sieve.

BIRIANI. (Fried Chicken.)

Cut a fowl into eight pieces, smear them with salt and pepper, and put to the one side for four hours;

after which wipe them and brown lightly in boiling ghee. When cold, smear all over (rubbing well in) with the following mixture :—one ounce of pounded cumin and coriander seeds, one-fifth of an ounce of caraway seeds, one ounce each of sugar and salt, and a quarter of an ounce of white pepper. Let this stand for ten minutes, and fry in the previously cooked ghee. Serve with chutnies, rice, or parautha.

PARAUTHA.

Make a good dough of wheaten flour and water, then work in some melted ghee and salt. Take small portions in the hands and roll them into balls, beat them into thin cakes, and fire on a flat piece of iron.

KABAB-I-TITER. (Roasted Partridges.)

First of all have the clean partridges stabbed all over with a sharp-pointed knife, rub in some ground salt and garam masalla, and let stand for four hours. After which fry them in two ounces of ghee till lightly browned all over. Mix the yolk of an egg with two ounces of thick milk curd, spread it on the bird, and roast in front of the fire. Chickens, pheasants, and guinea-fowls may be cooked the same way.

The recipe for garam masalla is in Brahmin recipe for farced potatoes.

KORMA. (Curried Mutton.)

Eight ounces of good thick milk curd, two tablespoonfuls of curry powder, a pinch of cayenne, five ounces of bruised sweet almonds, two or three bay leaves, a tablespoonful of water, the juice of five lemons, twelve large onions cut lengthwise into fine slices, three-quarters of a pound of butter or ghee, and a teaspoonful of salt.

Cut two pounds of good fat mutton into pieces an inch square. Fry the sliced onions in half of the ghee, and put in another dish; then fry the curry powder and pepper in the pan with the ghee. When quite brown, throw in the mutton and salt, and allow the whole to brown, after which add the water, spices, pepper, and bay leaves, the lemon juice, and the fried onions finely chopped; close the pot and allow it to simmer over a gentle fire for about an hour and a half or two hours, by which time the mutton will be quite ready. When just about finished, remove the bay leaves and add the rest of the ghee; then put in the milk curd, which must be good and thick, giving it all a stir round, and finish cooking. Eat with kachauri (lentil croquettes), rice, and chutnies.

KACHAURI. (Lentil Croquettes.)

Make some cakes the same as in "Puri," but not so large. Steep some lentils overnight, first washing them thoroughly, then boil in the water they were steeped in. Fry a chopped onion in boiling ghee till nicely coloured; strain the lentils and mix with the fried onions and ghee; season with some ground cinnamon, coriander, pepper, and salt. Stew for a few minutes, and when cold put a small quantity in the centre of one of the cakes and put another on top, being careful to wet the edges. Press down all round, and fry in boiling ghee. These are served hot in winter and cold in summer.

MANGO CHUTNEE.

Peel and slice fifty green mangoes, stone two pounds of tamarinds, three pounds of sugar boiled in one quart and a half of vinegar, a dessertspoonful and a half of cinnamon, one pound of salt, one pound of sliced green ginger, one teaspoonful of bruised garlic, a teaspoonful of red pepper, a half dessertspoonful of ground nutmeg, one pound of cleaned sultana raisins, and a quart and a half of vinegar.

Having sliced very finely the peeled mangoes, steep them for at least thirty-six hours in dry salt, after which clean the salt all away and boil them in the vinegar. Now remove to another pan (brass for preference), and mix all the ingredients (when the mangoes and vinegar are cold). Place on the fire and simmer for half an hour; you must add the syrup gradually, being careful to mix when adding. Keep stirring till all the liquor has been well absorbed. When stone cold, bottle and tie down with pieces of thin skin over the corks.

PALAO. (Pillau of Kid.)

Take four pounds of rice, one pound and a quarter of melted ghee or butter, eight ounces of onions, two ounces of salt, eight ounces of milk curd, two pounds of a well-grown kid, one ounce of cloves, and one ounce of cardamoms (unground).

Soak the rice in water, changing the water three times, and let it remain in the water for half an hour. Cut the onion into thin slices, and fry in boiling ghee or butter to a light brown. Cut the meat into small pieces and fry in the ghee. Add the salt and the curd, and stew till half cooked; ; then put in two pounds of water, the cloves, the cardamoms, the rice, and fried onions (which have been ground or well bruised). Stew the whole until quite cooked, which will be in about two hours. Eat with maize cakes (papar) and chutnies.

PAPAR. (Maize Cakes Spiced.)

Make a dough of finely ground maize flour and water ; season with a little cloves, cinnamon, black pepper, and salt. Roll out extremely thin, and cut into rounds and shapes of various sizes, and fry in boiling ghee.

BITE KELIA. (Baked Banana and Cocoanut.)

Take a teacupful of grated cocoanut and fry it till quite brown in a little ghee. Now stir in a few small cardamoms, a pinch of saffron, a teacupful of sugar, and sufficient rose water to make a soft mass when the sugar is melted.

Peel, slice through the middle longwise, and cut into two-inch lengths three bananas ; put them on a dish in which you have poured one ounce of melted ghee ;

cover thickly with the above mixture, and push into a moderate oven till the pieces of bananas are soft.

Apples, pears, peaches, apricots, cherries, and plums may be cooked in the same way.

ROTRI. (Sweetened Milk.)

Reduce four pounds of milk by boiling to a fourth of its original weight, then sweeten with sugar.

MOTICHOOR LADDOO. (Spiced Sugar Balls.)

Sift four pounds powdered gram (very small beans), and to this are added one and a half ounces of ghee and half an ounce of salt. These are mixed, and enough water added to form a batter capable of pouring.

A kettle containing two and a half pounds of ghee is put on a very gentle fire and allowed to boil. The batter already prepared is poured into a perforated ladle and allowed to fall through the holes in the form of globules into the boiling ghee. These at once solidify, and are removed with another perforated ladle, and set to the one side. Make a strong syrup of two and a half pounds of water and five and a half pounds of sugar, The whole mass of pellets is put into the solution of sugar and mixed. Cardamoms, cloves, and almonds are added. The mass is then wrought with the hands into the form of balls about the size of a small orange.

ZARDA. (Sweet Rice.)

Take one pound three ounces of rice, wash it twice, and keep it in water for an hour. Then make a syrup of twelve ounces of sugar in six ounces of water.

Put three ounces of ghee in a pan, also four cloves and six ounces of water. When the water boils put in the rice, and when the water dries up put thirty grains of saffron in the syrup already prepared, and mix it with the rice. Stir it with a spoon, and when the syrup is dried mix in four ounces of milk. Take the juice of an orange along with the juice of three prunes, which have been first steeped for some time in water, and pour it into the rice, and cook till rice is soft.

RABBRI. (Curdled Milk and Fruit.)

Have two pounds six ounces of milk boiled slowly, and have the cream put aside by a spoon. When the milk is reduced to nearly four ounces remove it, and mix up all the cream with it. When it becomes cool, mix in two ounces of sugar, forty-five grains of small cardamoms, and some almonds, pistachio nuts, and raisins.

PHIRNI. (Rice Sweet.)

A quantity of ground rice is soaked in water for twelve hours, and afterwards mixed in sixteen times the quantity of milk, to which is added a quantity of sugar double the quantity of rice. The mixture is then placed in a pan on the fire, and stirred until it becomes somewhat thick in the process of boiling. Mix in some small black cardamoms and little pieces of pine-apple, one for each of the cups. It is then poured into small cups of brass which, when cooled, are covered with exquisitely thin silver leaves on which chopped pistachios are sprinkled. The silver leaves are also eaten.

AMRITI. (Vanilla Tablet.)

Take a pound of ghee, melt it in a pot, stir in eight ounces of gram flour, four ounces of sugar, and four ounces of milk curd. Boil for a few minutes, stirring all the time. Remove from the fire, add some essence of vanilla, and beat till thick and creamy.

BALUSHAI. (Orange Tablet.)

Boil quarter of a pound of ghee, the same quantity of thick curd, and one pound of sugar, till it balls when you take a piece between the fingers. Remove from the fire, flavour with essence of orange, colour with a touch of saffron, and beat till it is thick and creamy. Pour into an oiled form and cut into handy pieces.

XX

RAJPUTANA (Brahmin)

Menu

Phulkā (Wheat Cakes)	Paranthā (Pastry Cakes)	Kachauri (Lentil Croquettes)
Ghol-Kā-Barā (Lentils and Curds)	Mitchā Chanvāl (Spiced Rice)	Ghi (Clarified Butter)
Phul Gobi (Cauliflower)	Aloo Kā Tarkāri (Potatoes)	Patta Gobi (Cabbage)
Sivayā Phirni (Sweet Spiced Vermicelli)	Zardā (Rice and Fruits)	Nukti (Sugar Balls)
Angir Murabbā (Fig Preserve)	Naringi Murabbā (Orange Preserve)	Shen Murabbā (Apple Preserve)

Kalākand
(Milk Sweets)

PHULKA. (Wheat Cakes.)

Mix wheatmeal and salt with water, and knead well. Divide into small portions, roll out; bake on a girdle, and when cooked spread with ghi or clarified butter, and rub one against the other. Eaten with all kinds of vegetables.

PARANTHA. (Pastry Cakes.)

Wheatmeal and salt. Mix in same way as phulki. Roll out, and put on pieces of clarified butter; fold, and roll out again. Again put on pieces of butter, fold, and roll out. Rub girdle well with clarified butter and cook on a flat piece of iron standing a little above the fire.

This is like puff paste, and mostly eaten with jams or preserved fruits.

KACHAURI. (Lentil Croquettes.)

Two pounds wheatmeal, half pound of clarified butter and salt. Mix all with water, knead well, roll into small balls, and flatten out with hand. Make small dents in the centre, into which put a little lentil paste (dal). Gather all together into a ball, flatten a little, and drop into boiling ghi or clarified butter, and cook.

Soak one pound of large lentils, and rub off the skin; grind it; add quarter salt-spoonful of red pepper and half a one of black; of big and little cardamoms, aniseed, black cumin seed, and salt of each a teaspoonful, and cook in water (very little) till a very thick paste.

Ghol-Ka-Bara. (Lentils and Curds.)

Clean and soak two pounds of lentils, and put in a pot with eight ounces of thick milk curd. Stir in a quarter saltspoonful of red pepper, half a teaspoonful of black pepper, a teaspoonful each of cinnamon, large cardamoms, little cardamoms, black cumin seeds, cloves, and cook till quite soft.

Mitcha Chanval. (Spiced Rice.)

Wash two pounds of rice and put in a pot with water, which should stand two inches above the rice. Stir in half a teaspoonful each of red chillies and black pepper, a teaspoonful each of cinnamon, cardamoms, aniseed, cumin, cloves, and sufficient saffron to give a good colour. Bring to the boil and simmer at the side of the fire till all the water is evaporated; but see that the rice is quite cooked, not pulpy, but all the grains separate.

Phul Gobi. (Cauliflower.)

Clean and break up cauliflower into small branches. Put into a pan some ghi or clarified butter. Chop a point of garlic and cook in this until red; add the vegetable and stir; add a little water, sufficient only to soak the vegetable. Add pepper and salt, cover, and stir occasionally to keep from burning.

Aloo Ka Tarkari. (Potatoes.)

Pare two pounds of potatoes, cut into small pieces and wash. Grind one teaspoonful of turmeric, same of cumin seed, quarter teaspoonful of garlic, and a salt-spoonful of white pepper; cook in ghi, stirring all the time. Put potatoes into this, add a little water and salt; cook until soft. Very little water is allowed.

PATTA GOBI. (Cabbage).

Cut a cabbage into small pieces. Cook two points sliced garlic in ghi until red. Add cabbage with a little water and salt; sufficient water only to make it soft. When soft and dry, remove garlic; pour over some melted ghi in which you have mixed a spoonful of coriander and cardamoms.

Most kinds of vegetables are cooked in this way.

SIVAYA PHIRNI. (Sweet Spiced Vermicelli).

Vermicilli may be used in place of sivaya.

Fry one pound of vermicelli in one pound of boiling ghi until it is a light brown. Stir in one ounce of rose water, one teaspoonful of peeled cardamoms and one pound of sugar; when the sugar is dissolved, add a tea-cupful of milk; give the mixture a stir, and simmer slowly at the side of the fire till dry.

ROTI NAN. (Sweet Cake.)

(*See* "Royal Dinner.")

ZAIDA. (Rice and Fruits.)

Two pounds of rice. Boil one pound of sugar till it threads on spoon. Wash the rice. Put in a pan some clarified butter with twelve cardamoms; add rice and stir for a little; add syrup and as much water as is necessary to cook the rice; colour with saffron; add two ounces each of chopped almonds, pistachios, ground cocoanut, and raisins. When rice is soft, take a fine cloth wrung out of water, put inside pan and cover with lid. Put to the side of the fire. This takes about fifteen minutes to cook.

NUKTI. (Sugar Balls.)

Make a paste of two pounds of fine flour of gram (the flour of the very small white pea will do), one pound of ghi, and a quarter ounce of salt; boil in a deep frying-pan two and a half lbs. of ghi; pour the paste with a cup into a strainer with big holes, and press it with a small pestle so as to get small round grains like peas into the boiling ghi. When cooked, remove them with a skimmer, and drain on a sieve till all the ghi is removed. Continue this process till all the paste is finished. The small grains are called boondi. Boil five pounds of sugar till nearly candy high and put the boondi in it, and make into balls as large as small apples.

ANGIR MARABBA. (Fig Preserve.)

Plump in hot water some figs till soft and clean; put them in a pot with plenty sugar syrup and a squeeze of lemon; boil till tender.

NARINGI MURABBA. (Orange Preserve.)

Skin six oranges, pare away all the pith, cut into slices, and remove pips, etc. Plump into boiling syrup (sufficient to cover them) for two or three minutes, and place in a dish with a little of the syrup.

SHEN MURABBA. (Apple Preserve.)

Thinly pare six apples, and core carefully. Put them into boiling syrup, adding some lemon juice and red colouring matter, and dish when tender but not too soft.

KALAKAND. (Milk Sweets.)

Boil equal quantities of milk and sugar until quite thick and creamy, and, when cold, cut in squares; decorate with silver and rose leaves.

XXI

RAJPUTANA (Royal)

Menu

Phulkā (Wheat Cakes)	Poori (Fried Cakes)	Shirmāl (Sweet Bread)
Chanvāl (Rice)	Dhāl (Spiced Lentils)	Ghi (Clarified Butter)
Pulav (Pillau of Mutton)	Pasundee (Fried Mutton)	Gourdā (Sheep's Kidneys)
Koftā (Chicken Balls)	Kalvā (Liver)	Khurmā (Curried Pork)

Phulki Laroo (Gram Pudding)

Naryal Pittās (Cocoanut Croquettes)

Rotri (Sweetened Milk)

Roti Nan (Sweet Cake)

Kabani Murabbā (Damson Preserve)	Rewund Murabba (Stewed Rhubarb)	Aru Murabbā (Peach Preserve)

Murg Pak (Melon Seeds)

Boat-kā-Hulva (Almond Sweet)

PHULKA. (Wheat Cakes.)

Make a good dough of wheat or maize meal, with water and a little salt. Knead well and roll out rather thin, and cut in small portions. Bake on a gridiron and immediately spread with ghi or clarified butter, and rest one against the other.

POORI. (Fried Cakes.)

Mix wheat meal and salt in same way as for phulki, Take small pieces, roll as thin as wafers, and cook in boiling ghi or clarified butter.

SHIRMAL. (Sweet Bread.)

Baked in the same way as ordinary household bread with yeast, adding raisins and sugar. Made in small cakes or like buns.

CHANVAL. (Rice.)

Wash two pounds of rice, and put in pot; cover it with two inches of water, bring to the boil, and stand on a slow fire to simmer till all the moisture is evaporated and the rice quite dry.

DAL. (Spiced Lentils.)

Wash lentils. Boil in water until soft. Put into a pan some ghi or clarified butter. Cook in this the following spices (ground) :—Cloves, garlic, cumin seed, turmeric, and salt and pepper. Add dal, and cook until soft. When ready, add more of the spices.

PULAV. (Pillau of Mutton.)

Fry eight ounces of sliced onions in eight ounces of boiling butter (ghi) till browned. Remove the onions to one side, and in the butter fry for a few minutes one pound of lean mutton cut in small pieces, and four ounces each of ground coriander seeds, cucumbers (gherkins) sliced, and green ginger, one ounce of garlic, a teaspoonful of salt, and a sliced red chilli. Put the meat in another pan along with four ounces of curds, half a stick of cinnamon broken into pieces, twelve large and twenty-four small cardamoms, an inch of mace broken into pieces, twelve whole cloves, and a little more salt. Simmer at the side of the fire till meat is tender. See that the pan is kept closely covered.

Wash twenty-four ounces of rice, and fry till slightly browned in eight ounces of ghi; then add another eight ounces of ghi, and cover closely, and stew till soft.

Take two pounds of the back ribs of mutton cut in small pieces, a few cloves, two ounces ginger, a point of garlic, and a little salt, and boil in sixty-four ounces of water till quite tender and the stock is reduced to twenty-four ounces. Strain and add to the two meats, fried onions and rice.

In another pan heat four ounces of ghi, and add two ounces each of sliced almonds, pistachio nuts, raisins, and a little cayenne pepper, a quarter ounce of musk, and the juice of two limes. Toss the pan till all are thoroughly heated, then add to the meats, etc., giving all a good stir to mix thoroughly. Hermetically close the lid of the pot, and stew very gently for fifteen or twenty minutes.

Pasundee. (Fried Mutton.)

Grind the following spices :—A teaspoonful of cumin seeds, half the quantity of cloves and cardamoms, with a seasoning of salt, black and red peppers. Cut mutton into long thin pieces. Rub spice well in, and fry in ghi or clarified butter till one side is cooked, then turn and fry the other side. Cover with onions cut in fine slices, which you had fried in the ghi before frying the mutton.

Gourda. (Sheeps' Kidneys.)

Skin, salt, and split six sheeps' kidneys, leaving the two halves attached. Prepare and cook the same as " Fried Mutton."

For the European table only use pepper and salt, and grill in front or over the fire. Served with grilled bacon to breakfast or luncheon.

Kofta. (Chicken Balls).

Take a raw minced chicken, pound it to a fine paste, season with a teaspoonful of ground coriander and salt, half the quantity of aniseed and red chillies. Mix with a little milk curd, make into balls, and fry in ghi or clarified butter.

Kalva. (Liver.)

Cut one pound of lamb or calf's liver into pieces about two inches square and quarter of an inch thick. Shred half a pound of onions, and brown in ghi ; add liver, and toss on fire till lightly browned. Add a teaspoonful each of ground coriander, turmeric, and aniseed, half the quantity of red chillies, and salt, a pinch of sugar, two ounces ghi, four ounces curd, and a cup of water. Simmer very slowly for two hours. There should be a good deal of gravy.

KHURMA. (Curried Pork).

Fry in four ounces of boiling ghi or butter eight ounces of finely shred onions, two ounces of sliced garlic, two ounces of whole cardamoms, two ounces of whole cloves, and a piece of mace* weighing about an ounce broken into pieces ; when onions are of a light brown, remove them.

Make a paste of four ounces each of ground coriander, cucumbers, green ginger, chillies (one third red and two thirds green), two points of garlic, a teaspoonful of salt, and four ounces of milk curd.

Take two pounds of tender pork and cut it into pieces about an inch square and half an inch thick. Put the meat into a pot along with fried condiments (leaving out the sliced garlic) and condiment paste, adding half a cupful of milk curd and a cupful of water ; cover closely, and stew very slowly from two to three hours, or till the meat is very tender. Just before dishing pour in four ounces each of sweet and sour curds, seven and a half grains of musk mixed with two ounces of hot ghi and a pinch of saffron to give a good colour. There should be a good deal of gravy.

*If leaf mace is unobtainable, use ½ oz. of powdered mace or nutmeg.

Beef, mutton, lamb, kid, venison, ducks, and chickens may be cooked the same way.

PHULKI LAROO. (Gram Pudding.)

Grind half a pound of gram (the very small brown bean will do) till it is the size of semolina: mix it with four ounces of ghi and half a pound of castor sugar. When the ghi and sugar are melted and well mixed with the flour by stirring them over the fire, add a pinch of cinnamon, one teaspoonful of ground cardamoms, and half a teacupful of milk curd; give a good stir round and simmer at the side of the fire till it is a soft moist mass. Take portions in the hands and mould into balls as large as tennis balls, on the top of which sprinkle finely sliced pistachios and sweet blanched almonds; or you may pour the mixture into a dish and spread the pistachios and almonds on top.

NARYAL PITTAS. (Cocoanut Croquettes.)

Put some finely scraped cocoanut into a pan along with some thick sugar syrup and a pinch of black cardamom powder. Fry till browned, but not charred, and place to the one side. Make a nice dough of finely sifted rice flour and boiling water; knead well. Take a piece of the dough as large as an egg and press it out flat with the hands to the size of a large saucer; put a tablespoonful of the cocoanut mixture in the centre, and fold over in the shape of a half moon; wet the edges and press them closely together. Tie a clean cloth over the top of a pot of boiling water, place the cakes on the top, and steam for half an hour.

ROTRI. (Sweetened Milk.)

Reduce four pounds of milk by boiling to a fourth of its original weight; then sweeten with plenty of sugar.

ROTI NAN. (Sweet Cake.)

Take twenty-four ounces of fine flour, and boil with milk until it becomes thick like dough, after which divide the boiled dough into five parts, and place them on a table. Take two ounces almonds, two ounces pistachio nuts, two ounces raisins, and one pound of milk boiled till it is reduced to four ounces, two ounces sugar, and mix these with a little butter (ghi), and fry till the mixture is browned. Pound the mixture until it is divided into little particles or pellets. Then mix the whole and add to this a little saffron, musk, and cardamoms, and put these in the brown mixture. Now take the dough and roll each of the five pieces into a separate bannock or cake, and pour a little melted butter over them. Then take the almond, sugar, and cardamom mixture and put a little in the middle of each cake, and put one cake on the top of the other, and press the sides together with a little water until all are completely closed up; but before doing so put a little condensed milk on the top, again closing the edges till all the five cakes are on the top of each other. Spread a little saffron on the topmost cake. When this is done, with a knife cut away the rough edges, and put in an oven with as much butter as will cover the cakes, and let them bake half an hour. See that they are well browned, and then pour off the melted butter. Ornament the top of the cake with icing sugar. When this is done, the cake can be cut into pieces and served up.

This cake is a particular favourite of His Highness the Maharana, and is always eaten at a Palace dinner.

KABANI MURABBA. (Damson Preserve.)

Boil equal quantities of damsons and sugar syrup till it jellies.

REWUND MURABBA. (Stewed Rhubarb).

Clean and cut sticks of rhubarb into two-inch lengths. Place the pieces in a pan. Cover closely and stew very gently at the side of the fire or in the oven till tender. After which pour in sufficient very strong sugar syrup to sweeten.

ARU MURABBA. (Peach Preserve.)

Skin the peaches, and cut a slit to take out the stones. Strew rather more than their weight of sugar over them, and stand till next day, when stew very slowly till they look clear, being careful to remove any scum. Remove the fruit and boil up the syrup, and pour it over the fruit ; do this three times at intervals of two days.

MURG PAK. (Melon Seeds.)

Take off outside skin from seeds. Put ghi (clarified butter) in pan, and cook seeds in this. Cook sugar with water until it threads from spoon. Add seeds to syrup, and beat till thick and creamy. Pour into a flat dish, and then cut in squares.

BOAT-KA-HULVA. (Almond Sweets.)

Take of ground almonds half a pound, sugar half a pound, cream (milk reduced to quarter its bulk by boiling) six ounces, saffron five grains, ghi four ounces, whole cardamoms half a dozen, and whole cloves one dozen.

Fry the cardamoms and cloves thoroughly in boiling ghi. Mix the ground almonds with the cream in a basin. Boil the sugar in a little water till it is very thick in consistency. Mix this with the almond paste, then add it to the ghi which you have brought to the boil; continue boiling for a quarter of an hour, stirring all the time. Remove from the fire and add the ground saffron; beat up very well till thick and creamy, then pour into a dish before it cools.

XXII

AFGHANISTAN

MENU

Sharbát
(Sherbet)

Shrini
(Sweets)

Kawah Chái (Cardamom Tea)	Chái (Plain Tea)
Pillau-i-Baráh (Pillau of Lamb)	Kaurmah-i-Ahú (Stewed Venison)
Kaurmah-i-gusht-i-gusfand (Curried Mutton)	Kaurmah-i-Chuchai Murgh (Stewed Chicken)

Pillau-i-Habáté
(Pillau of Vegetables)

Halwa Nasháshta
(Arrowroot Pudding)

Tázeh Mivah
(Fresh Fruits)

Kawah Chái (Cardamom Tea)	Chái (Plain Tea)

Kakullah Chai. (Cardamom Tea.)

Infuse some Indian tea along with a few cardamoms, and at same time put in plenty of sugar syrup. The tea has to be very weak, very sweet, and very strongly flavoured with cardamoms.

Two cups have to be taken, thereafter a cup of plain tea is taken to correct the palate.

Leavened Brown Bread.

Prepare a sponge with four pounds of whole meal (half wheat and half rye), two ounces of butter, a little salt, and three ounces of yeast, and sufficient luke-warm water to make a nice size of dough. Set the dough to rise for one hour ; then knead it well, form it into shapes (if for this country, put into tins), and bake in a good oven If for Europeans all the meal must be wheat.

Yeast.

Boil half a pound of flour, 2 ounces of brown sugar, and a little salt in one gallon of water for an hour. Remove from the fire, and when blood-warm put it into bottles and close tight for future use. Half a pint will make 9 pounds of bread.

Unleavened Brown Bread.

Mix well half-ounce of soda, half-ounce of cream of tartar, with two pounds of whole wheat meal ; put it out on a table or baking board, make a space in the centre, and put into it a teaspoonful of salt, add about a pint of water, then mix all together into a smooth dough, form it into shapes, and bake in a good oven.

Omit soda, cream of tartar, and salt for Eastern bread ; if for Afghanistan, use rye instead of wheat.

Pillau-i-Rarah. (Pillau of Lamb.)

Slice a couple of onions (medium) and fry in half a pound of boiling butter. Cut two pounds of lamb in bits about the size of a square inch, fry these in the butter for a few minutes ; then put the onions, butter, and meat in a stewpan along with half-a-dozen dried apricots and a handful of pistachio nuts, a teaspoonful each of ground turmeric, cummin, coriander, and half that quantity of ground caraway and cloves, and a large chilli sliced, with salt to taste. Pour in one cupful of water and one of milk curds, and stew very slowly for four hours. Serve in a dish surrounded with boiled rice.

Boiled Rice.

Wash three cupfuls of rice and plunge into boiling water, and boil fiercely for twenty minutes till rice cooked but firm. Drain off the water very thoroughly and put back into the pot with a good piece of butter, first rubbing the pot with butter before returning the rice. Place in the oven or at the side of the fire to dry. Turn over the rice occasionally very lightly, so that each grain may be separate.

Kaurmah-i-Ahu. (Stewed Venison.)

Cut two pounds of vension into small pieces and fry in half a pound of butter in which you have first fried a couple of minced onions. Place the whole into a pan with six stoned peaches, a cupful of raisins, twelve sweet prunes (stoned), a cupful of pine cone seeds, a teaspoonful each of ground cinnamon, green ginger, sugar, two sliced green chillies, and salt and pepper to taste. Mix all well together, and pour in three cupfuls of sour milk and one of melted butter, and stew very slowly for at least four hours. Serve with buttered beetroots and brown bread.

Buttered Beetroots.

Wash two pounds of beetroots very carefully, taking care not to break the skin, or they will bleed. Boil in salted water with some corriander leaves and a couple of bay leaves and a teaspoonful of whole peppers. When tender, take them out of the water and skin very carefully. Cut them into nice pieces, heat a pound of butter, and put them into it, and stew for half an hour.

When for European cookery, cut them into thin slices, place in a jar and pour boiling spiced vinegar over, and in a couple of days you have pickled beetroot.

Pillau-i-Habâté. (Pillau of Vegetables.)

Boil any kind of vegetables in season, such as potatoes, artichokes, cauliflower, cucumbers, carrots, pumpkins, and vegetable marrows. Strain the vegetables and put to one side.

Melt, say, three ounces of butter, and, when boiling, fry two onions sliced very fine, and when brown, but not charred, make the following into a paste, and fry in the butter, viz. :—A teaspoonful each of mustard seeds, turmeric, and chillies, a quarter of a teaspoonful of garlic, and three corriander leaves. When smoothly made into a paste and fried, put in a cupful of milk curd, 6 ounces of butter, and when all is amalgamated pour the whole over the vegetables, which you have first put into another pan. Mix thoroughly, and simmer for twenty minutes. Dish up and surround with rice.

KAURMAH-I-GUSHT-I-GUSFAND. (Curried Mutton.)

Fry a couple of minced onions in butter. Cut up two pounds of mutton into small pieces and fry in the butter. Place the whole in a stewpan with a teaspoonful each of ground corriander, cummin, cardamoms, green ginger, a point of garlic, and two large red chillies sliced, a dozen stoned sour plums, a handful of raisins, and half a teaspoonful of salt. Stew very slowly for four hours, and eat with new bread, boiled rice, and buttered parsnips.

BUTTERED PARSNIPS.

Thoroughly clean the roots and cut into pieces of about two inches long and half-an-inch thick, boil in salted water, and, when tender, drain and put them into another pot with plenty of butter and stew for half an hour.

For European cookery they must be mashed and beaten up with a good bit of butter and some cream. Season with pepper and salt to taste.

Kaurmah-i-Chuchai Murgh. (Stewed Chicken.)

Lightly fry two medium-sized onions sliced very thin in half a pound of boiling butter. Remove the onions and fry in the butter a plump chicken; when brown all over place it in a pan, add the onions, a handful of pounded almonds, four oranges which have been preserved in sugar syrup, and cut in quarters, a teaspoonful each of ground cardamoms, cinnamon, half a teaspoonful of nutmeg, two bay leaves, two sliced chillies, a teaspoonful of salt, and quarter that quantity of white pepper. Pour into the pan another half-pound of melted butter and a cupful of milk curds. Cover very closely and stew for at least four hours. Remove the bay leaves and eat with brown bread.

Preserved Oranges.

Wash and dry half a dozen oranges. Cut a very thin piece out of the rind, about the thickness of a thin cord, as if you were quartering them. Boil them in plenty of water till they are quite tender, then cut them into the quarters already marked off; cut out the pips and the hard bits of pith; boil in plenty of strong sugar syrup for half an hour; let them steep in the syrup for four days, then boil for fifteen minutes, and do this four times; strain into another pot and add more syrup and boil to a crackling point and pour over the oranges. When cold, tie down very carefully.

Halwa Nashashta. (Arrowroot Pudding.)

Half a pound of arrowroot, half a pound of butter, half a pound of sugar, and one pint of water. Soak the arrowroot in half of the water, when nearly soft drain it, and put it in a pot in which you have brought the butter to boiling point; stir continually till all the butter is absorbed with the arrowroot. Having made a clear syrup of the sugar and the rest of the water, add it to the mixture and cook steadily, stirring all the time very carefully, but not shaking the pot. When all has collected into a mass, lift it with a spoon several times till it is quite free and smooth. It ought to be a soft, solid mass. Eat with all kinds of fruits preserved in sweet syrups.

Sharbat. (Sherbet.)

Boil the juice of six oranges and one lemon, also the very thin rind of three of the oranges and one of the lemons with an equal weight of sugar for ten minutes. Strain and set to cool on ice; dilute with a little rose water and fill up with iced water to taste.

A CATALOGUE OF SELECTED DOVER BOOKS
IN ALL FIELDS OF INTEREST

A CATALOGUE OF SELECTED DOVER BOOKS IN ALL FIELDS OF INTEREST

THE NOTEBOOKS OF LEONARDO DA VINCI, edited by J.P. Richter. Extracts from manuscripts reveal great genius; on painting, sculpture, anatomy, sciences, geography, etc. Both Italian and English. 186 ms. pages reproduced, plus 500 additional drawings, including studies for Last Supper, Sforza monument, etc. 860pp. 7⅞ x 10¾. USO 22572-0, 22573-9 Pa., Two vol. set $12.00

ART NOUVEAU DESIGNS IN COLOR, Alphonse Mucha, Maurice Verneuil, Georges Auriol. Full-color reproduction of Combinaisons ornamentales (c. 1900) by Art Nouveau masters. Floral, animal, geometric, interlacings, swashes — borders, frames, spots — all incredibly beautiful. 60 plates, hundreds of designs. 9⅜ x 8¹⁄₁₆. 22885-1 Pa. $4.00

GRAPHIC WORKS OF ODILON REDON. All great fantastic lithographs, etchings, engravings, drawings, 209 in all. Monsters, Huysmans, still life work, etc. Introduction by Alfred Werner. 209pp. 9⅛ x 12¼. 21996-8 Pa. $5.00

EXOTIC FLORAL PATTERNS IN COLOR, E.-A. Seguy. Incredibly beautiful full-color pochoir work by great French designer of 20's. Complete Bouquets et frondaisons, Suggestions pour étoffes. Richness must be seen to be believed. 40 plates containing 120 patterns. 80pp. 9⅜ x 12¼. 23041-4 Pa. $6.00

SELECTED ETCHINGS OF JAMES A. MCN. WHISTLER, James A. McN. Whistler. 149 outstanding etchings by the great American artist, including selections from the Thames set and two Venice sets, the complete French set, and many individual prints. Introduction and explanatory note on each print by Maria Naylor. 157pp. 9⅜ x 12¼. 23194-1 Pa. $5.00

VISUAL ILLUSIONS: THEIR CAUSES, CHARACTERISTICS, AND APPLICATIONS, Matthew Luckiesh. Thorough description, discussion; shape and size, color, motion; natural illusion. Uses in art and industry. 100 illustrations. 252pp. 21530-X Pa. $2.50

TEN BOOKS ON ARCHITECTURE, Vitruvius. The most important book ever written on architecture. Early Roman aesthetics, technology, classical orders, site selection, all other aspects. Stands behind everything since. Morgan translation. 331pp. 20645-9 Pa. $3.50

THE CODEX NUTTALL, A PICTURE MANUSCRIPT FROM ANCIENT MEXICO, as first edited by Zelia Nuttall. Only inexpensive edition, in full color, of a pre-Columbian Mexican (Mixtec) book. 88 color plates show kings, gods, heroes, temples, sacrifices. New explanatory, historical introduction by Arthur G. Miller. 96pp. 11⅜ x 8½. 23168-2 Pa. $7.50

CREATIVE LITHOGRAPHY AND HOW TO DO IT, Grant Arnold. Lithography as art form: working directly on stone, transfer of drawings, lithotint, mezzotint, color printing; also metal plates. Detailed, thorough. 27 illustrations. 214pp. 21208-4 Pa. $3.00

DESIGN MOTIFS OF ANCIENT MEXICO, Jorge Enciso. Vigorous, powerful ceramic stamp impressions — Maya, Aztec, Toltec, Olmec. Serpents, gods, priests, dancers, etc. 153pp. 6[1]/8 x 9¼. 20084-1 Pa. $2.50

AMERICAN INDIAN DESIGN AND DECORATION, Leroy Appleton. Full text, plus more than 700 precise drawings of Inca, Maya, Aztec, Pueblo, Plains, NW Coast basketry, sculpture, painting, pottery, sand paintings, metal, etc. 4 plates in color. 279pp. 8⅜ x 11¼. 22704-9 Pa. $4.50

CHINESE LATTICE DESIGNS, Daniel S. Dye. Incredibly beautiful geometric designs: circles, voluted, simple dissections, etc. Inexhaustible source of ideas, motifs. 1239 illustrations. 469pp. 6⅛ x 9¼. 23096-1 Pa. $5.00

JAPANESE DESIGN MOTIFS, Matsuya Co. Mon, or heraldic designs. Over 4000 typical, beautiful designs: birds, animals, flowers, swords, fans, geometric; all beautifully stylized. 213pp. 11⅜ x 8¼. 22874-6 Pa. $4.95

PERSPECTIVE, Jan Vredeman de Vries. 73 perspective plates from 1604 edition; buildings, townscapes, stairways, fantastic scenes. Remarkable for beauty, surrealistic atmosphere; real eye-catchers. Introduction by Adolf Placzek. 74pp. 11⅜ x 8¼. 20186-4 Pa. $2.75

EARLY AMERICAN DESIGN MOTIFS, Suzanne E. Chapman. 497 motifs, designs, from painting on wood, ceramics, appliqué, glassware, samplers, metal work, etc. Florals, landscapes, birds and animals, geometrics, letters, etc. Inexhaustible. Enlarged edition. 138pp. 8⅜ x 11¼. 22985-8 Pa. $3.50
23084-8 Clothbd. $7.95

VICTORIAN STENCILS FOR DESIGN AND DECORATION, edited by E.V. Gillon, Jr. 113 wonderful ornate Victorian pieces from German sources; florals, geometrics; borders, corner pieces; bird motifs, etc. 64pp. 9⅜ x 12¼. 21995-X Pa. $2.50

ART NOUVEAU: AN ANTHOLOGY OF DESIGN AND ILLUSTRATION FROM THE STUDIO, edited by E.V. Gillon, Jr. Graphic arts: book jackets, posters, engravings, illustrations, decorations; Crane, Beardsley, Bradley and many others. Inexhaustible. 92pp. 8⅛ x 11. 22388-4 Pa. $2.50

ORIGINAL ART DECO DESIGNS, William Rowe. First-rate, highly imaginative modern Art Deco frames, borders, compositions, alphabets, florals, insectals, Wurlitzer-types, etc. Much finest modern Art Deco. 80 plates, 8 in color. 8⅜ x 11¼. 22567-4 Pa. $3.00

HANDBOOK OF DESIGNS AND DEVICES, Clarence P. Hornung. Over 1800 basic geometric designs based on circle, triangle, square, scroll, cross, etc. Largest such collection in existence. 261pp. 20125-2 Pa. $2.50

150 MASTERPIECES OF DRAWING, edited by Anthony Toney. 150 plates, early 15th century to end of 18th century; Rembrandt, Michelangelo, Dürer, Fragonard, Watteau, Wouwerman, many others. 150pp. 8³/₈ x 11¼. 21032-4 Pa. $3.50

THE GOLDEN AGE OF THE POSTER, Hayward and Blanche Cirker. 70 extraordinary posters in full colors, from Maîtres de l'Affiche, Mucha, Lautrec, Bradley, Cheret, Beardsley, many others. 9³/₈ x 12¼. 22753-7 Pa. $4.95
21718-3 Clothbd. $7.95

SIMPLICISSIMUS, selection, translations and text by Stanley Appelbaum. 180 satirical drawings, 16 in full color, from the famous German weekly magazine in the years 1896 to 1926. 24 artists included: Grosz, Kley, Pascin, Kubin, Kollwitz, plus Heine, Thöny, Bruno Paul, others. 172pp. 8½ x 12¼. 23098-8 Pa. $5.00
23099-6 Clothbd. $10.00

THE EARLY WORK OF AUBREY BEARDSLEY, Aubrey Beardsley. 157 plates, 2 in color: Manon Lescaut, Madame Bovary, Morte d'Arthur, Salome, other. Introduction by H. Marillier. 175pp. 8½ x 11. 21816-3 Pa. $3.50

THE LATER WORK OF AUBREY BEARDSLEY, Aubrey Beardsley. Exotic masterpieces of full maturity: Venus and Tannhäuser, Lysistrata, Rape of the Lock, Volpone, Savoy material, etc. 174 plates, 2 in color. 176pp. 8½ x 11. 21817-1 Pa. $3.75

DRAWINGS OF WILLIAM BLAKE, William Blake. 92 plates from Book of Job, Divine Comedy, Paradise Lost, visionary heads, mythological figures, Laocoön, etc. Selection, introduction, commentary by Sir Geoffrey Keynes. 178pp. 8½ x 11. 22303-5 Pa. $3.50

LONDON: A PILGRIMAGE, Gustave Doré, Blanchard Jerrold. Squalor, riches, misery, beauty of mid-Victorian metropolis; 55 wonderful plates, 125 other illustrations, full social, cultural text by Jerrold. 191pp. of text. 8¹/₈ x 11. 22306-X Pa. $5.00

THE COMPLETE WOODCUTS OF ALBRECHT DÜRER, edited by Dr. W. Kurth. 346 in all: Old Testament, St. Jerome, Passion, Life of Virgin, Apocalypse, many others. Introduction by Campbell Dodgson. 285pp. 8½ x 12¼. 21097-9 Pa. $6.00

THE DISASTERS OF WAR, Francisco Goya. 83 etchings record horrors of Napoleonic wars in Spain and war in general. Reprint of 1st edition, plus 3 additional plates. Introduction by Philip Hofer. 97pp. 9³/₈ x 8¼. 21872-4 Pa. $2.50

ENGRAVINGS OF HOGARTH, William Hogarth. 101 of Hogarth's greatest works: Rake's Progress, Harlot's Progress, Illustrations for Hudibras, Midnight Modern Conversation, Before and After, Beer Street and Gin Lane, many more. Full commentary. 256pp. 11 x 14. 22479-1 Pa. $6.00
23023-6 Clothbd. $13.50

PRIMITIVE ART, Franz Boas. Great anthropologist on ceramics, textiles, wood, stone, metal, etc.; patterns, technology, symbols, styles. All areas, but fullest on Northwest Coast Indians. 350 illustrations. 378pp. 20025-6 Pa. $3.50

CONSTRUCTION OF AMERICAN FURNITURE TREASURES, Lester Margon. 344 detail drawings, complete text on constructing exact reproductions of 38 early American masterpieces: Hepplewhite sideboard, Duncan Phyfe drop-leaf table, mantel clock, gate-leg dining table, Pa. German cupboard, more. 38 plates. 54 photographs. 168pp. 8³/8 x 11¼. 23056-2 Pa. $4.00

JEWELRY MAKING AND DESIGN, Augustus F. Rose, Antonio Cirino. Professional secrets revealed in thorough, practical guide: tools, materials, processes; rings, brooches, chains, cast pieces, enamelling, setting stones, etc. Do not confuse with skimpy introductions: beginner can use, professional can learn from it. Over 200 illustrations. 306pp. 21750-7 Pa. $3.00

METALWORK AND ENAMELLING, Herbert Maryon. Generally conceded best all-around book. Countless trade secrets: materials, tools, soldering, filigree, setting, inlay, niello, repoussé, casting, polishing, etc. For beginner or expert. Author was foremost British expert. 330 illustrations. 335pp. 22702-2 Pa. $3.50

WEAVING WITH FOOT-POWER LOOMS, Edward F. Worst. Setting up a loom, beginning to weave, constructing equipment, using dyes, more, plus over 285 drafts of traditional patterns including Colonial and Swedish weaves. More than 200 other figures. For beginning and advanced. 275pp. 8¾ x 6³/8. 23064-3 Pa. $4.00

WEAVING A NAVAJO BLANKET, Gladys A. Reichard. Foremost anthropologist studied under Navajo women, reveals every step in process from wool, dyeing, spinning, setting up loom, designing, weaving. Much history, symbolism. With this book you could make one yourself. 97 illustrations. 222pp. 22992-0 Pa. $3.00

NATURAL DYES AND HOME DYEING, Rita J. Adrosko. Use natural ingredients: bark, flowers, leaves, lichens, insects etc. Over 135 specific recipes from historical sources for cotton, wool, other fabrics. Genuine premodern handicrafts. 12 illustrations. 160pp. 22688-3 Pa. $2.00

THE HAND DECORATION OF FABRICS, Francis J. Kafka. Outstanding, profusely illustrated guide to stenciling, batik, block printing, tie dyeing, freehand painting, silk screen printing, and novelty decoration. 356 illustrations. 198pp. 6 x 9. 21401-X Pa. $3.00

THOMAS NAST: CARTOONS AND ILLUSTRATIONS, with text by Thomas Nast St. Hill. Father of American political cartooning. Cartoons that destroyed Tweed Ring; inflation, free love, church and state; original Republican elephant and Democratic donkey; Santa Claus; more. 117 illustrations. 146pp. 9 x 12.
22983-1 Pa. $4.00
23067-8 Clothbd. $8.50

FREDERIC REMINGTON: 173 DRAWINGS AND ILLUSTRATIONS. Most famous of the Western artists, most responsible for our myths about the American West in its untamed days. Complete reprinting of *Drawings of Frederic Remington* (1897), plus other selections. 4 additional drawings in color on covers. 140pp. 9 x 12. 20714-5 Pa. $3.95

EARLY NEW ENGLAND GRAVESTONE RUBBINGS, Edmund V. Gillon, Jr. 43 photographs, 226 rubbings show heavily symbolic, macabre, sometimes humorous primitive American art. Up to early 19th century. 207pp. 8³/₈ x 11¼.
21380-3 Pa. $4.00

L.J.M. DAGUERRE: THE HISTORY OF THE DIORAMA AND THE DAGUERREOTYPE, Helmut and Alison Gernsheim. Definitive account. Early history, life and work of Daguerre; discovery of daguerreotype process; diffusion abroad; other early photography. 124 illustrations. 226pp. 6¹/₆ x 9¼. 22290-X Pa. $4.00

PHOTOGRAPHY AND THE AMERICAN SCENE, Robert Taft. The basic book on American photography as art, recording form, 1839-1889. Development, influence on society, great photographers, types (portraits, war, frontier, etc.), whatever else needed. Inexhaustible. Illustrated with 322 early photos, daguerreotypes, tintypes, stereo slides, etc. 546pp. 6¹/₈ x 9¼. 21201-7 Pa. $5.00

PHOTOGRAPHIC SKETCHBOOK OF THE CIVIL WAR, Alexander Gardner. Reproduction of 1866 volume with 100 on-the-field photographs: Manassas, Lincoln on battlefield, slave pens, etc. Introduction by E.F. Bleiler. 224pp. 10¾ x 9.
22731-6 Pa. $4.50

THE MOVIES: A PICTURE QUIZ BOOK, Stanley Appelbaum & Hayward Cirker. Match stars with their movies, name actors and actresses, test your movie skill with 241 stills from 236 great movies, 1902-1959. Indexes of performers and films. 128pp. 8³/₈ x 9¼. 20222-4 Pa. $2.50

THE TALKIES, Richard Griffith. Anthology of features, articles from Photoplay, 1928-1940, reproduced complete. Stars, famous movies, technical features, fabulous ads, etc.; Garbo, Chaplin, King Kong, Lubitsch, etc. 4 color plates, scores of illustrations. 327pp. 8³/₈ x 11¼. 22762-6 Pa. $5.95

THE MOVIE MUSICAL FROM VITAPHONE TO "42ND STREET," edited by Miles Kreuger. Relive the rise of the movie musical as reported in the pages of Photoplay magazine (1926-1933): every movie review, cast list, ad, and record review; every significant feature article, production still, biography, forecast, and gossip story. Profusely illustrated. 367pp. 8³/₈ x 11¼. 23154-2 Pa. $6.95

JOHANN SEBASTIAN BACH, Philipp Spitta. Great classic of biography, musical commentary, with hundreds of pieces analyzed. Also good for Bach's contemporaries. 450 musical examples. Total of 1799pp.
EUK 22278-0, 22279-9 Clothbd., Two vol. set $25.00

BEETHOVEN AND HIS NINE SYMPHONIES, Sir George Grove. Thorough history, analysis, commentary on symphonies and some related pieces. For either beginner or advanced student. 436 musical passages. 407pp. 20334-4 Pa. $4.00

MOZART AND HIS PIANO CONCERTOS, Cuthbert Girdlestone. The only full-length study. Detailed analyses of all 21 concertos, sources; 417 musical examples. 509pp. 21271-8 Pa. $4.50

THE FITZWILLIAM VIRGINAL BOOK, edited by J. Fuller Maitland, W.B. Squire. Famous early 17th century collection of keyboard music, 300 works by Morley, Byrd, Bull, Gibbons, etc. Modern notation. Total of 938pp. 8³/₈ x 11.
ECE 21068-5, 21069-3 Pa., Two vol. set $12.00

COMPLETE STRING QUARTETS, Wolfgang A. Mozart. Breitkopf and Härtel edition. All 23 string quartets plus alternate slow movement to K156. Study score. 277pp. 9³/₈ x 12¼.
22372-8 Pa. $6.00

COMPLETE SONG CYCLES, Franz Schubert. Complete piano, vocal music of Die Schöne Müllerin, Die Winterreise, Schwanengesang. Also Drinker English singing translations. Breitkopf and Härtel edition. 217pp. 9³/₈ x 12¼.
22649-2 Pa. $4.00

THE COMPLETE PRELUDES AND ETUDES FOR PIANOFORTE SOLO, Alexander Scriabin. All the preludes and etudes including many perfectly spun miniatures. Edited by K.N. Igumnov and Y.I. Mil'shteyn. 250pp. 9 x 12.
22919-X Pa. $5.00

TRISTAN UND ISOLDE, Richard Wagner. Full orchestral score with complete instrumentation. Do not confuse with piano reduction. Commentary by Felix Mottl, great Wagnerian conductor and scholar. Study score. 655pp. 8¹/₈ x 11.
22915-7 Pa. $10.00

FAVORITE SONGS OF THE NINETIES, ed. Robert Fremont. Full reproduction, including covers, of 88 favorites: Ta-Ra-Ra-Boom-De-Aye, The Band Played On, Bird in a Gilded Cage, Under the Bamboo Tree, After the Ball, etc. 401pp. 9 x 12.
EBE 21536-9 Pa. $6.95

SOUSA'S GREAT MARCHES IN PIANO TRANSCRIPTION: ORIGINAL SHEET MUSIC OF 23 WORKS, John Philip Sousa. Selected by Lester S. Levy. Playing edition includes: The Stars and Stripes Forever, The Thunderer, The Gladiator, King Cotton, Washington Post, much more. 24 illustrations. 111pp. 9 x 12.
USO 23132-1 Pa. $3.50

CLASSIC PIANO RAGS, selected with an introduction by Rudi Blesh. Best ragtime music (1897-1922) by Scott Joplin, James Scott, Joseph F. Lamb, Tom Turpin, 9 others. Printed from best original sheet music, plus covers. 364pp. 9 x 12.
EBE 20469-3 Pa. $6.95

ANALYSIS OF CHINESE CHARACTERS, C.D. Wilder, J.H. Ingram. 1000 most important characters analyzed according to primitives, phonetics, historical development. Traditional method offers mnemonic aid to beginner, intermediate student of Chinese, Japanese. 365pp.
23045-7 Pa. $4.00

MODERN CHINESE: A BASIC COURSE, Faculty of Peking University. Self study, classroom course in modern Mandarin. Records contain phonetics, vocabulary, sentences, lessons. 249 page book contains all recorded text, translations, grammar, vocabulary, exercises. Best course on market. 3 12" 33⅓ monaural records, book, album.
98832-5 Set $12.50

THE BEST DR. THORNDYKE DETECTIVE STORIES, R. Austin Freeman. The Case of Oscar Brodski, The Moabite Cipher, and 5 other favorites featuring the great scientific detective, plus his long-believed-lost first adventure — 31 New Inn — reprinted here for the first time. Edited by E.F. Bleiler. USO 20388-3 Pa. $3.00

BEST "THINKING MACHINE" DETECTIVE STORIES, Jacques Futrelle. The Problem of Cell 13 and 11 other stories about Prof. Augustus S.F.X. Van Dusen, including two "lost" stories. First reprinting of several. Edited by E.F. Bleiler. 241pp. 20537-1 Pa. $3.00

UNCLE SILAS, J. Sheridan LeFanu. Victorian Gothic mystery novel, considered by many best of period, even better than Collins or Dickens. Wonderful psychological terror. Introduction by Frederick Shroyer. 436pp. 21715-9 Pa. $4.00

BEST DR. POGGIOLI DETECTIVE STORIES, T.S. Stribling. 15 best stories from EQMM and The Saint offer new adventures in Mexico, Florida, Tennessee hills as Poggioli unravels mysteries and combats Count Jalacki. 217pp. 23227-1 Pa. $3.00

EIGHT DIME NOVELS, selected with an introduction by E.F. Bleiler. Adventures of Old King Brady, Frank James, Nick Carter, Deadwood Dick, Buffalo Bill, The Steam Man, Frank Merriwell, and Horatio Alger — 1877 to 1905. Important, entertaining popular literature in facsimile reprint, with original covers. 190pp. 9 x 12. 22975-0 Pa. $3.50

ALICE'S ADVENTURES UNDER GROUND, Lewis Carroll. Facsimile of ms. Carroll gave Alice Liddell in 1864. Different in many ways from final Alice. Handlettered, illustrated by Carroll. Introduction by Martin Gardner. 128pp. 21482-6 Pa. $1.50

ALICE IN WONDERLAND COLORING BOOK, Lewis Carroll. Pictures by John Tenniel. Large-size versions of the famous illustrations of Alice, Cheshire Cat, Mad Hatter and all the others, waiting for your crayons. Abridged text. 36 illustrations. 64pp. 8¼ x 11. 22853-3 Pa. $1.50

AVENTURES D'ALICE AU PAYS DES MERVEILLES, Lewis Carroll. Bué's translation of "Alice" into French, supervised by Carroll himself. Novel way to learn language. (No English text.) 42 Tenniel illustrations. 196pp. 22836-3 Pa. $2.00

MYTHS AND FOLK TALES OF IRELAND, Jeremiah Curtin. 11 stories that are Irish versions of European fairy tales and 9 stories from the Fenian cycle — 20 tales of legend and magic that comprise an essential work in the history of folklore. 256pp. 22430-9 Pa. $3.00

EAST O' THE SUN AND WEST O' THE MOON, George W. Dasent. Only full edition of favorite, wonderful Norwegian fairytales — Why the Sea is Salt, Boots and the Troll, etc. — with 77 illustrations by Kittelsen & Werenskiöld. 418pp. 22521-6 Pa. $3.50

PERRAULT'S FAIRY TALES, Charles Perrault and Gustave Doré. Original versions of Cinderella, Sleeping Beauty, Little Red Riding Hood, etc. in best translation, with 34 wonderful illustrations by Gustave Doré. 117pp. 8⅛ x 11. 22311-6 Pa. $2.50

MOTHER GOOSE'S MELODIES. Facsimile of fabulously rare Munroe and Francis "copyright 1833" Boston edition. Familiar and unusual rhymes, wonderful old woodcut illustrations. Edited by E.F. Bleiler. 128pp. 4½ x 6⅜. 22577-1 Pa. $1.00

MOTHER GOOSE IN HIEROGLYPHICS. Favorite nursery rhymes presented in rebus form for children. Fascinating 1849 edition reproduced in toto, with key. Introduction by E.F. Bleiler. About 400 woodcuts. 64pp. 6⅞ x 5¼. 20745-5 Pa. $1.00

PETER PIPER'S PRACTICAL PRINCIPLES OF PLAIN & PERFECT PRONUNCIATION. Alliterative jingles and tongue-twisters. Reproduction in full of 1830 first American edition. 25 spirited woodcuts. 32pp. 4½ x 6⅜. 22560-7 Pa. $1.00

MARMADUKE MULTIPLY'S MERRY METHOD OF MAKING MINOR MATHEMATICIANS. Fellow to Peter Piper, it teaches multiplication table by catchy rhymes and woodcuts. 1841 Munroe & Francis edition. Edited by E.F. Bleiler. 103pp. 4⅝ x 6.
22773-1 Pa. $1.25
20171-6 Clothbd. $3.00

THE NIGHT BEFORE CHRISTMAS, Clement Moore. Full text, and woodcuts from original 1848 book. Also critical, historical material. 19 illustrations. 40pp. 4⅝ x 6. 22797-9 Pa. $1.00

THE KING OF THE GOLDEN RIVER, John Ruskin. Victorian children's classic of three brothers, their attempts to reach the Golden River, what becomes of them. Facsimile of original 1889 edition. 22 illustrations. 56pp. 4⅝ x 6⅜.
20066-3 Pa. $1.25

DREAMS OF THE RAREBIT FIEND, Winsor McCay. Pioneer cartoon strip, unexcelled for beauty, imagination, in 60 full sequences. Incredible technical virtuosity, wonderful visual wit. Historical introduction. 62pp. 8⅜ x 11¼. 21347-1 Pa. $2.00

THE KATZENJAMMER KIDS, Rudolf Dirks. In full color, 14 strips from 1906-7; full of imagination, characteristic humor. Classic of great historical importance. Introduction by August Derleth. 32pp. 9¼ x 12¼. 23005-8 Pa. $2.00

LITTLE ORPHAN ANNIE AND LITTLE ORPHAN ANNIE IN COSMIC CITY, Harold Gray. Two great sequences from the early strips: our curly-haired heroine defends the Warbucks' financial empire and, then, takes on meanie Phineas P. Pinchpenny. Leapin' lizards! 178pp. 6⅛ x 8⅜. 23107-0 Pa. $2.00

WHEN A FELLER NEEDS A FRIEND, Clare Briggs. 122 cartoons by one of the greatest newspaper cartoonists of the early 20th century — about growing up, making a living, family life, daily frustrations and occasional triumphs. 121pp. 8½ x 9½.
23148-8 Pa. $2.50

THE BEST OF GLUYAS WILLIAMS. 100 drawings by one of America's finest cartoonists: The Day a Cake of Ivory Soap Sank at Proctor & Gamble's, At the Life Insurance Agents' Banquet, and many other gems from the 20's and 30's. 118pp. 8⅜ x 11¼. 22737-5 Pa. $2.50

THE MAGIC MOVING PICTURE BOOK, Bliss, Sands & Co. The pictures in this book move! Volcanoes erupt, a house burns, a serpentine dancer wiggles her way through a number. By using a specially ruled acetate screen provided, you can obtain these and 15 other startling effects. Originally "The Motograph Moving Picture Book." 32pp. 8¼ x 11. 23224-7 Pa. $1.75

STRING FIGURES AND HOW TO MAKE THEM, Caroline F. Jayne. Fullest, clearest instructions on string figures from around world: Eskimo, Navajo, Lapp, Europe, more. Cats cradle, moving spear, lightning, stars. Introduction by A.C. Haddon. 950 illustrations. 407pp. 20152-X Pa. $3.00

PAPER FOLDING FOR BEGINNERS, William D. Murray and Francis J. Rigney. Clearest book on market for making origami sail boats, roosters, frogs that move legs, cups, bonbon boxes. 40 projects. More than 275 illustrations. Photographs. 94pp. 20713-7 Pa. $1.25

INDIAN SIGN LANGUAGE, William Tomkins. Over 525 signs developed by Sioux, Blackfoot, Cheyenne, Arapahoe and other tribes. Written instructions and diagrams: how to make words, construct sentences. Also 290 pictographs of Sioux and Ojibway tribes. 111pp. 6⅛ x 9¼. 22029-X Pa. $1.50

BOOMERANGS: HOW TO MAKE AND THROW THEM, Bernard S. Mason. Easy to make and throw, dozens of designs: cross-stick, pinwheel, boomabird, tumblestick, Australian curved stick boomerang. Complete throwing instructions. All safe. 99pp. 23028-7 Pa. $1.50

25 KITES THAT FLY, Leslie Hunt. Full, easy to follow instructions for kites made from inexpensive materials. Many novelties. Reeling, raising, designing your own. 70 illustrations. 110pp. 22550-X Pa. $1.25

TRICKS AND GAMES ON THE POOL TABLE, Fred Herrmann. 79 tricks and games, some solitaires, some for 2 or more players, some competitive; mystifying shots and throws, unusual carom, tricks involving cork, coins, a hat, more. 77 figures. 95pp. 21814-7 Pa. $1.25

WOODCRAFT AND CAMPING, Bernard S. Mason. How to make a quick emergency shelter, select woods that will burn immediately, make do with limited supplies, etc. Also making many things out of wood, rawhide, bark, at camp. Formerly titled Woodcraft. 295 illustrations. 580pp. 21951-8 Pa. $4.00

AN INTRODUCTION TO CHESS MOVES AND TACTICS SIMPLY EXPLAINED, Leonard Barden. Informal intermediate introduction: reasons for moves, tactics, openings, traps, positional play, endgame. Isolates patterns. 102pp. USO 21210-6 Pa. $1.35

LASKER'S MANUAL OF CHESS, Dr. Emanuel Lasker. Great world champion offers very thorough coverage of all aspects of chess. Combinations, position play, openings, endgame, aesthetics of chess, philosophy of struggle, much more. Filled with analyzed games. 390pp. 20640-8 Pa. $3.50

HOW TO SOLVE CHESS PROBLEMS, Kenneth S. Howard. Practical suggestions on problem solving for very beginners. 58 two-move problems, 46 3-movers, 8 4-movers for practice, plus hints. 171pp. 20748-X Pa. $2.00

A GUIDE TO FAIRY CHESS, Anthony Dickins. 3-D chess, 4-D chess, chess on a cylindrical board, reflecting pieces that bounce off edges, cooperative chess, retrograde chess, maximummers, much more. Most based on work of great Dawson. Full handbook, 100 problems. 66pp. 7⅞ x 10¾. 22687-5 Pa. $2.00

WIN AT BACKGAMMON, Millard Hopper. Best opening moves, running game, blocking game, back game, tables of odds, etc. Hopper makes the game clear enough for anyone to play, and win. 43 diagrams. 111pp. 22894-0 Pa. $1.50

BIDDING A BRIDGE HAND, Terence Reese. Master player "thinks out loud" the binding of 75 hands that defy point count systems. Organized by bidding problem—no-fit situations, overbidding, underbidding, cueing your defense, etc. 254pp. EBE 22830-4 Pa. $2.50

THE PRECISION BIDDING SYSTEM IN BRIDGE, C.C. Wei, edited by Alan Truscott. Inventor of precision bidding presents average hands and hands from actual play, including games from 1969 Bermuda Bowl where system emerged. 114 exercises. 116pp. 21171-1 Pa. $1.75

LEARN MAGIC, Henry Hay. 20 simple, easy-to-follow lessons on magic for the new magician: illusions, card tricks, silks, sleights of hand, coin manipulations, escapes, and more —all with a minimum amount of equipment. Final chapter explains the great stage illusions. 92 illustrations. 285pp. 21238-6 Pa. $2.95

THE NEW MAGICIAN'S MANUAL, Walter B. Gibson. Step-by-step instructions and clear illustrations guide the novice in mastering 36 tricks; much equipment supplied on 16 pages of cut-out materials. 36 additional tricks. 64 illustrations. 159pp. 6⅝ x 10. 23113-5 Pa. $3.00

PROFESSIONAL MAGIC FOR AMATEURS, Walter B. Gibson. 50 easy, effective tricks used by professionals —cards, string, tumblers, handkerchiefs, mental magic, etc. 63 illustrations. 223pp. 23012-0 Pa. $2.50

CARD MANIPULATIONS, Jean Hugard. Very rich collection of manipulations; has taught thousands of fine magicians tricks that are really workable, eye-catching. Easily followed, serious work. Over 200 illustrations. 163pp. 20539-8 Pa. $2.00

ABBOTT'S ENCYCLOPEDIA OF ROPE TRICKS FOR MAGICIANS, Stewart James. Complete reference book for amateur and professional magicians containing more than 150 tricks involving knots, penetrations, cut and restored rope, etc. 510 illustrations. Reprint of 3rd edition. 400pp. 23206-9 Pa. $3.50

THE SECRETS OF HOUDINI, J.C. Cannell. Classic study of Houdini's incredible magic, exposing closely-kept professional secrets and revealing, in general terms, the whole art of stage magic. 67 illustrations. 279pp. 22913-0 Pa. $2.50

DRIED FLOWERS, Sarah Whitlock and Martha Rankin. Concise, clear, practical guide to dehydration, glycerinizing, pressing plant material, and more. Covers use of silica gel. 12 drawings. Originally titled "New Techniques with Dried Flowers." 32pp. 21802-3 Pa. $1.00

ABC OF POULTRY RAISING, J.H. Florea. Poultry expert, editor tells how to raise chickens on home or small business basis. Breeds, feeding, housing, laying, etc. Very concrete, practical. 50 illustrations. 256pp. 23201-8 Pa. $3.00

HOW INDIANS USE WILD PLANTS FOR FOOD, MEDICINE & CRAFTS, Frances Densmore. Smithsonian, Bureau of American Ethnology report presents wealth of material on nearly 200 plants used by Chippewas of Minnesota and Wisconsin. 33 plates plus 122pp. of text. 6⅛ x 9¼. 23019-8 Pa. $2.50

THE HERBAL OR GENERAL HISTORY OF PLANTS, John Gerard. The 1633 edition revised and enlarged by Thomas Johnson. Containing almost 2850 plant descriptions and 2705 superb illustrations, Gerard's Herbal is a monumental work, the book all modern English herbals are derived from, and the one herbal every serious enthusiast should have in its entirety. Original editions are worth perhaps $750. 1678pp. 8½ x 12¼. 23147-X Clothbd. $50.00

A MODERN HERBAL, Margaret Grieve. Much the fullest, most exact, most useful compilation of herbal material. Gigantic alphabetical encyclopedia, from aconite to zedoary, gives botanical information, medical properties, folklore, economic uses, and much else. Indispensable to serious reader. 161 illustrations. 888pp. 6½ x 9¼. USO 22798-7, 22799-5 Pa., Two vol. set $10.00

HOW TO KNOW THE FERNS, Frances T. Parsons. Delightful classic. Identification, fern lore, for Eastern and Central U.S.A. Has introduced thousands to interesting life form. 99 illustrations. 215pp. 20740-4 Pa. $2.50

THE MUSHROOM HANDBOOK, Louis C.C. Krieger. Still the best popular handbook. Full descriptions of 259 species, extremely thorough text, habitats, luminescence, poisons, folklore, etc. 32 color plates; 126 other illustrations. 560pp. 21861-9 Pa. $4.50

HOW TO KNOW THE WILD FRUITS, Maude G. Peterson. Classic guide covers nearly 200 trees, shrubs, smaller plants of the U.S. arranged by color of fruit and then by family. Full text provides names, descriptions, edibility, uses. 80 illustrations. 400pp. 22943-2 Pa. $3.00

COMMON WEEDS OF THE UNITED STATES, U.S. Department of Agriculture. Covers 220 important weeds with illustration, maps, botanical information, plant lore for each. Over 225 illustrations. 463pp. 6⅛ x 9¼. 20504-5 Pa. $4.50

HOW TO KNOW THE WILD FLOWERS, Mrs. William S. Dana. Still best popular book for East and Central USA. Over 500 plants easily identified, with plant lore; arranged according to color and flowering time. 174 plates. 459pp. 20332-8 Pa. $3.50

MANUAL OF THE TREES OF NORTH AMERICA, Charles S. Sargent. The basic survey of every native tree and tree-like shrub, 717 species in all. Extremely full descriptions, information on habitat, growth, locales, economics, etc. Necessary to every serious tree lover. Over 100 finding keys. 783 illustrations. Total of 986pp.
20277-1, 20278-X Pa., Two vol. set $8.00

BIRDS OF THE NEW YORK AREA, John Bull. Indispensable guide to more than 400 species within a hundred-mile radius of Manhattan. Information on range, status, breeding, migration, distribution trends, etc. Foreword by Roger Tory Peterson. 17 drawings; maps. 540pp. 23222-0 Pa. $6.00

THE SEA-BEACH AT EBB-TIDE, Augusta Foote Arnold. Identify hundreds of marine plants and animals: algae, seaweeds, squids, crabs, corals, etc. Descriptions cover food, life cycle, size, shape, habitat. Over 600 drawings. 490pp.
21949-6 Pa. $4.00

THE MOTH BOOK, William J. Holland. Identify more than 2,000 moths of North America. General information, precise species descriptions. 623 illustrations plus 48 color plates show almost all species, full size. 1968 edition. Still the basic book. Total of 551pp. 6½ x 9¼. 21948-8 Pa. $6.00

AN INTRODUCTION TO THE REPTILES AND AMPHIBIANS OF THE UNITED STATES, Percy A. Morris. All lizards, crocodiles, turtles, snakes, toads, frogs; life history, identification, habits, suitability as pets, etc. Non-technical, but sound and broad. 130 photos. 253pp. 22982-3 Pa. $3.00

OLD NEW YORK IN EARLY PHOTOGRAPHS, edited by Mary Black. Your only chance to see New York City as it was 1853-1906, through 196 wonderful photographs from N.Y. Historical Society. Great Blizzard, Lincoln's funeral procession, great buildings. 228pp. 9 x 12. 22907-6 Pa. $6.00

THE AMERICAN REVOLUTION, A PICTURE SOURCEBOOK, John Grafton. Wonderful Bicentennial picture source, with 411 illustrations (contemporary and 19th century) showing battles, personalities, maps, events, flags, posters, soldier's life, ships, etc, all captioned and explained. A wonderful browsing book, supplement to other historical reading. 160pp. 9 x 12. 23226-3 Pa. $4.00

PERSONAL NARRATIVE OF A PILGRIMAGE TO AL-MADINAH AND MECCAH, Richard Burton. Great travel classic by remarkably colorful personality. Burton, disguised as a Moroccan, visited sacred shrines of Islam, narrowly escaping death. Wonderful observations of Islamic life, customs, personalities. 47 illustrations. Total of 959pp. 21217-3, 21218-1 Pa., Two vol. set $7.00

INCIDENTS OF TRAVEL IN CENTRAL AMERICA, CHIAPAS, AND YUCATAN, John L. Stephens. Almost single-handed discovery of Maya culture; exploration of ruined cities, monuments, temples; customs of Indians. 115 drawings. 892pp.
22404-X, 22405-8 Pa., Two vol. set $8.00

HOUDINI ON MAGIC, Harold Houdini. Edited by Walter Gibson, Morris N. Young. How he escaped; exposés of fake spiritualists; instructions for eye-catching tricks; other fascinating material by and about greatest magician. 155 illustrations. 280pp. 20384-0 Pa. $2.50

HANDBOOK OF THE NUTRITIONAL CONTENTS OF FOOD, U.S. Dept. of Agriculture. Largest, most detailed source of food nutrition information ever prepared. Two mammoth tables: one measuring nutrients in 100 grams of edible portion; the other, in edible portion of 1 pound as purchased. Originally titled Composition of Foods. 190pp. 9 x 12. 21342-0 Pa. $4.00

COMPLETE GUIDE TO HOME CANNING, PRESERVING AND FREEZING, U.S. Dept. of Agriculture. Seven basic manuals with full instructions for jams and jellies; pickles and relishes; canning fruits, vegetables, meat; freezing anything. Really good recipes, exact instructions for optimal results. Save a fortune in food. 156 illustrations. 214pp. 6⅛ x 9¼. 22911-4 Pa. $2.50

THE BREAD TRAY, Louis P. De Gouy. Nearly every bread the cook could buy or make: bread sticks of Italy, fruit breads of Greece, glazed rolls of Vienna, everything from corn pone to croissants. Over 500 recipes altogether. including buns, rolls, muffins, scones, and more. 463pp. 23000-7 Pa. $3.50

CREATIVE HAMBURGER COOKERY, Louis P. De Gouy. 182 unusual recipes for casseroles, meat loaves and hamburgers that turn inexpensive ground meat into memorable main dishes: Arizona chili burgers, burger tamale pie, burger stew, burger corn loaf, burger wine loaf, and more. 120pp. 23001-5 Pa. $1.75

LONG ISLAND SEAFOOD COOKBOOK, J. George Frederick and Jean Joyce. Probably the best American seafood cookbook. Hundreds of recipes. 40 gourmet sauces, 123 recipes using oysters alone! All varieties of fish and seafood amply represented. 324pp. 22677-8 Pa. $3.00

THE EPICUREAN: A COMPLETE TREATISE OF ANALYTICAL AND PRACTICAL STUDIES IN THE CULINARY ART, Charles Ranhofer. Great modern classic. 3,500 recipes from master chef of Delmonico's, turn-of-the-century America's best restaurant. Also explained, many techniques known only to professional chefs. 775 illustrations. 1183pp. 6⅝ x 10. 22680-8 Clothbd. $17.50

THE AMERICAN WINE COOK BOOK, Ted Hatch. Over 700 recipes: old favorites livened up with wine plus many more: Czech fish soup, quince soup, sauce Perigueux, shrimp shortcake, filets Stroganoff, cordon bleu goulash, jambonneau, wine fruit cake, more. 314pp. 22796-0 Pa. $2.50

DELICIOUS VEGETARIAN COOKING, Ivan Baker. Close to 500 delicious and varied recipes: soups, main course dishes (pea, bean, lentil, cheese, vegetable, pasta, and egg dishes), savories, stews, whole-wheat breads and cakes, more. 168pp. USO 22834-7 Pa. $1.75

COOKIES FROM MANY LANDS, Josephine Perry. Crullers, oatmeal cookies, chaux au chocolate, English tea cakes, mandel kuchen, Sacher torte, Danish puff pastry, Swedish cookies — a mouth-watering collection of 223 recipes. 157pp.
22832-0 Pa. $2.00

ROSE RECIPES, Eleanour S. Rohde. How to make sauces, jellies, tarts, salads, potpourris, sweet bags, pomanders, perfumes from garden roses; all exact recipes. Century old favorites. 95pp. 22957-2 Pa. $1.25

"OSCAR" OF THE WALDORF'S COOKBOOK, Oscar Tschirky. Famous American chef reveals 3455 recipes that made Waldorf great; cream of French, German, American cooking, in all categories. Full instructions, easy home use. 1896 edition. 907pp. 6⅝ x 9⅜. 20790-0 Clothbd. $15.00

JAMS AND JELLIES, May Byron. Over 500 old-time recipes for delicious jams, jellies, marmalades, preserves, and many other items. Probably the largest jam and jelly book in print. Originally titled May Byron's Jam Book. 276pp.
USO 23130-5 Pa. $3.00

MUSHROOM RECIPES, André L. Simon. 110 recipes for everyday and special cooking. Champignons à la grecque, sole bonne femme, chicken liver croustades, more; 9 basic sauces, 13 ways of cooking mushrooms. 54pp.
USO 20913-X Pa. $1.25

FAVORITE SWEDISH RECIPES, edited by Sam Widenfelt. Prepared in Sweden, offers wonderful, clearly explained Swedish dishes: appetizers, meats, pastry and cookies, other categories. Suitable for American kitchen. 90 photos. 157pp.
23156-9 Pa. $2.00

THE BUCKEYE COOKBOOK, Buckeye Publishing Company. Over 1,000 easy-to-follow, traditional recipes from the American Midwest: bread (100 recipes alone), meat, game, jam, candy, cake, ice cream, and many other categories of cooking. 64 illustrations. From 1883 enlarged edition. 416pp. 23218-2 Pa. $4.00

TWENTY-TWO AUTHENTIC BANQUETS FROM INDIA, Robert H. Christie. Complete, easy-to-do recipes for almost 200 authentic Indian dishes assembled in 22 banquets. Arranged by region. Selected from Banquets of the Nations. 192pp.
23200-X Pa. $2.50

Prices subject to change without notice.
Available at your book dealer or write for free catalogue to Dept. GI, Dover Publications, Inc., 180 Varick St., N.Y., N.Y. 10014. Dover publishes more than 150 books each year on science, elementary and advanced mathematics, biology, music, art, literary history, social sciences and other areas.